Racia Discrimin Against Black Teachers and Black Professionals in the Pittsburgh Public School System: 1834-1973

Ralph Proctor, Jr.

Social Context Series

Learning Moments Press
Oakmont, PA

Racial Discrimination Against Black Teachers and Professionals
in the Pittsburgh Public School System: 1834-1973
Published by Learning Moments Press
Social Context Series
Oakmont, PA 15139
scholarpractitionernexus.com

ISBN-13 978-1-7349594-4-4

BISAC Subject:
Education/History (EDU 016000)
History/Social History (HIS 054000)
Social Science/Ethic Studies/American/African American & Black Studies (SOC 001000)
Social Science/Discrimination (SOC 031000)
Social Science/Race & Ethic Relations (SOC 070000)
Education/Multicultural Education (EDU020000)
Political Science/Civil Rights (POL004000)

Onix Audience Code: 06 Professional & Scholarly

Book Layout: Mike Murray, pearhouse.com

Photographs courtesy of the Carnegie Museum of Art,
Charles "Teenie" Harris Archive © 2014

Charles "Teenie" Harris

Helen Elizabeth Smith Faison
June 1946

In 1983, Faison became a deputy superintendent, making her the school district's highest-ranking woman. And when she led the school district as interim superintendent from early 1999 to mid-2000, she was the first African American to do so. (*Pitt Chronicle,* July 27, 2015).

Christine Jones Fulwylie, Teacher – 1968

Jody Harris, Teacher *(on left)* **- 1940-1950**

Table of Contents

Publisher's Note 3

Dedication 5

Prologue 7

Preface.. 11

Chapter 1 – The Wall of Discrimination.............................. 15

Chapter 2 – The First Black Teachers in Pittsburgh 27

Chapter 3 – External Pressure:
The Cracks in the Wall 59

Chapter 4 – Internal Pressure:
More Blacks in Professional Positions 121

Chapter 5 – Concluding Summary 147

Information Sources... 151

Acknowledgements... 155

About the Author 157

Publisher's Note

In writing his Prologue, Dr. Proctor commented that he received some pressure to publish his dissertation, a pressure he resisted for a number of years. "After all," he said, "the original was available." Despite his disinclination to publish, Learning Moments Press is pleased to make Dr. Proctor's research available for three reasons.

First and foremost, Proctor's account of racism toward Black professionals provides an important historical context for those who are part of the profession of education. Without understanding these historical roots, we run the risk of perpetuating discriminatory policies and practices. As the COVID 19 pandemic made all too apparent, major inequities exist between schools districts in affluent and poverty-riven communities. Legislation like *Brown v Board of Education* does little to create true equality in public education if individuals cling, consciously or unconsciously, to racist values. Publishing this book is done with the hope that it will be more accessible for use as a classroom text in courses such as the social foundations of education, education and society, and multicultural education.

The second reason for publishing the book is related to Dr. Proctor's struggle to pursue a method of inquiry that was not acknowledged as legitimate at the University of Pittsburgh much before 1980. The resistance he encountered in the Department of History was similar to that encountered among doctoral students in the University's School of Education. In all fairness, these struggles within the context of one university mirrored struggles that were occurring in academic institutions throughout the United States. The precepts of traditional scientific inquiry were being challenged in a number of fields of study where the focus was on the complexities of human meaning-making within complex social communities. Just a few years after Proctor finished his dissertation, it became a common practice to state as clearly as possible the position or perspective from which one was studying a phenomenon. While scientists stated their perspectives in terms of limitations and delimitations of a study, those working in interpretive fields of inquiry (what is often called "qualitative" research) described the socio-economic, ethnic, and gendered lenses through which they made their interpretations and drew their conclusions. Proctor's work foreshadows this inquiry convention that had begun to emerge just as he began his dissertation.

Third, Learning Moments Press is dedicated to providing examples of inquiry that are embedded in lived experience. This dedication stems from a conviction that individuals who engage thoughtfully and rigorously in inquiries are able to provide insights into the dilemmas that challenge professional practitioners. Pursuing such inquiries often entails a passionate commitment to make visible that which is hidden among taken-for-granted assumptions. Ralph Proctor has dedicated his life to just such a passionate pursuit in the name of civil liberties and social justice. His work deserves to be made visible, just as he makes visible the trials and triumphs of Black educators.

Dedication

This book is dedicated to many people who made contributions to my life that cannot be overstated. First are my parents, Ralph and Ruby Proctor, whose love sustained me through all life's tribulations; who demanded no more than that I do my best.

It is also dedicated to my sons, Shawn and Vance Proctor. All that I have done in life was to make the path easier for you. Thank you for being there. Thank you for your love.

To the teachers featured in this book and to the countless others who suffered the indignities described in this book but continued so that I and many other Black youngsters understood the value of the great education with which you provided us: thank you. Your work paved the way for the success of thousands of Black youth. Like a pebble tossed onto the surface of a still pond, the concentric circles continue to expand beyond the far horizons.

To Art Tuden and Morton "Moe" Coleman, who continued to provide support and comfort throughout the years for all my efforts and who always worked to convince me that what I was doing, in documenting the lives of Black folks, was truly important: thank you, my friends. You departed this Earth far too soon.

To my long-time friend, Patricia Buddemeyer, without whose help this project and others in my life would never have been completed: thank you from the bottom of my heart. Your friendship has been a sustaining force in my life.

There are, of course others to whom I owe a great debt. I will not embarrass you by exposing you in the pages but you know who you are. There is no need to put down your names. I have thanked you many times before.

Hazel Stallings *(seated at piano)* **with 5th grade music class at Vann Elementary – September 1959**

Lawrence Peeler, Among the 1st Black teachers hired by Pittsburgh Public Schools, taught choral and instrumental music – October 30, 1941

Prologue

This book was born out of battle and frustration, many years ago. I was an ABD (all but dissertation) student at the University of Pittsburgh and struggling to find a subject that was so narrowly focused that no other human being had ever explored the subject. This was a firm requirement of my department. I finally recalled stories of frustration I had been told many times when I was in elementary school. These stories were of African American school teachers who were educated in Pittsburgh but had begun their teaching careers someplace else. I occasionally wondered about that, but never took the time to explore the issue. Now, faced with finding a subject for which there was no documentation, I decided to focus on racial discrimination against Black teachers in my own home town. The literature search required of all PhD candidates showed that almost nothing existed about the subject.

I tried to find documentation for the subject in the files of the Pittsburgh Board of Public Education but was told repeatedly that no such information existed. I knew this was not true, because several White former administrators from the Board had specifically given me the name of the person who had the information. Frustrated by such blatant stonewalling, I was about to give up when a close friend smiled, suggested I try one more time, and mention her name at the beginning of my next call. Suddenly, the information magically became available. Later my friend told me the information gatekeeper had been one of her high school teachers, an important lesson in the intricacies of research beyond the library.

With the Board of Education hurdle behind me, I next faced the challenge of gathering the information I needed. What written information existed had not been formally published. I found myself hunched over musty old boxes of papers at The Archives of an Industrial Society in Hillman Library at the University of Pittsburgh. As I sneezed and coughed my way through this treasure trove, I found unpublished manuscripts that told of a "colored school" system in Pittsburgh. I spent many a weary hour deciphering faded, almost illegible hand-written notes of the minutes of Pittsburgh Board of Education meetings. But locked in those pages was much information that had never been seen by the public. In the 1970s when I was conducting this historical study, computers were not available to student researchers. The internet had not been invented. So I had no choice but to spend almost an entire summer with my head in microfilm machines, reading newspapers and other documents.

Although I was amassing a cache of documents, they did not tell the full story. What remained elusive was the process that led to Black people, who had been trained and educated in Pittsburgh and who were qualified to teach, having to leave Pittsburgh to pursue their chosen field. I had heard the story again and again, but I needed to understand how this happened. Who was responsible? How was it started? Why did the policy exist in a city that was supposedly free of racial discrimination? It occurred to me that all of the information I needed was locked in the minds of older Black teachers and other key players in the battle for civil rights in Pittsburgh. All I had to do was to talk to people, record their responses and use that information as the basis for my dissertation. EASY! Or so I thought.

I shared my strategy with my dissertation chairman and other faculty in the history department. I was surprised when they advised me to use the "standard" process for a dissertation—i.e., immersing myself in so-called "primary sources" such as newspapers, magazine articles, dissertations, and other printed material. I argued that none of these were "primary" because they were, essentially, "reports" written by observers. I was also expected to translate something from a comparative field of study and a specialty field of study related to American History, my major field of study.[1] None of this made sense

---

1   At the time, it did not occur to me to argue that Black language could constitute a "second" language that I was uniquely positioned to translate and interpret. Since then linguistic scholars have given much attention to the characteristic styles of expression used among Blacks within their communities and those used when interacting within White contexts. Further, I might have argued that print and broadcast journalism constituted comparative fields of study. At the time I was doing my doctoral research, such ideas would have seemed quite radical at the University of Pittsburgh (and at many major research institutions in the United States).

to me, but I had to comply with most of it. However, I dug my heels in on the use of primary sources, arguing for a technique called "oral history."

I based my argument on three points. One, the official "primary" sources were the experiences of the individuals who had suffered from discriminatory policies and practices, not the accounts written by those with a vested interest in denying the existence of racism. White individuals who admitted to me that racist practices did exist, had never been asked to document their assertions.

Two, in an irony apparently unnoticed by a number of faculty, I was accused of being too lazy or too unintelligent to do "normal" research— the same type of racist judgments to which the Black teachers I wanted to study had been subjected. In rebuttal, I drew upon the concept of "oral history." In a tradition stretching back thousands of years, story tellers were the keepers of history for people who had no written language. I drew upon the more recent work of Louis "Studs" Terkel, a pioneer "oral historian" who was audio-recording the voices of the ordinary and the extraordinary people throughout the world.[2] I argued I was at least as competent in gathering oral histories as Terkel, because I had spent more than ten years on radio and television, perfecting the art of interviewing.[3]

Three, having experience as a newspaper reporter and an editor of a black community newspaper, I had developed techniques for verifying the first person accounts that people told me.[4] Because of this work, I was respected within the Black community and, therefore, in a position

---

2　Studs Terkel was an award-winning author. Among his many books are *Working: People Talk about What They Do All Day and How They Feel about What They Do*; *"The Good War": An Oral History of World War II*; *Hard Times: An Oral History of the Great Depression*; *Race: How Blacks and Whites Think and Feel about the American Obsession*.

3　I hosted *Black Horizons* on Pittsburgh's public radio; the second such program in the United States.

4　I had worked for The Pittsburgh Courier as a contributing reporter, photographer, and editor.

to gather information that might not be shared with outsiders who would be viewed with suspicion.[5]

In the end, I won the argument and received approval—with considerable faculty skepticism—to use oral history as a research method. After successfully defending my dissertation, I began to receive calls from professors who had begun to use my work and wanted additional information. Years later, in another ironic twist, I received a phone call from one of the History department secretaries who had witnessed my dissertation battle. The department had used my work to secure a major grant to set up an Oral History Project. And, irony upon irony, a White male with no experience in oral history, was hired to run the program. So, the racism I had proved reared its ugly head once again.

The World Since 1973

Pressure continued to mount against the Pittsburgh Board of Public Education by members of the Pittsburgh Civil Rights Movement. Change since then has been slow as Black folks battled to get a Black superintendent. That did not happen until 1999. Battles continued, as well, to get more Blacks on the Board of Directors of the school system. Despite the fact that most of the students attending the Pittsburgh Public Schools were African American, the Board continued to be controlled by White folks for many years. So, the struggle for equality in the Pittsburgh Public Schools continues. More research must be conducted to document the continuing saga of racial discrimination in The Pittsburgh Public School system. But that is a job for much younger folks. Proctor OUT!!!

---

5   The issue of establishing trust and rapport with potential research participants has been a subject of great concern in the social sciences. In the early years of anthropology and sociology, in an effort to remain "objective," researchers tried to maintain enough distance to avoid "going native"—i.e., identifying too closely or strongly with the often "exotic" cultures and societies they were studying as outsiders. Over the years, it became increasingly apparent that the researchers were anything but "objective," as they interpreted what they were observing through their own culturally biased lenses. In the years since I completed my dissertation, a great deal has been written on the subject on procedures that respect the integrity of research participants' "stories," and the dilemmas associated with the retelling of others' stories.

Preface

This book is a publication of a study that traced the changing nature of racial discrimination against Black teachers and professionals in the Pittsburgh Public School system from 1834 to 1973. Even though a significant number of Blacks lived in Pittsburgh since the early 19th century and Black children have constituted a large percentage of the public school population since World War I, Blacks have been repeatedly discriminated against when seeking employment in the Pittsburgh Public School system. In fact, Blacks were totally excluded from teaching in Pittsburgh Public Schools between 1881 and 1933.

A great many Pittsburghers, especially those who have been involved in the civil rights and human rights struggle, are generally aware of this discrimination. Yet, at the time this study was undertaken, there had been no systematic study of the scope and type of discrimination Black teachers and professionals faced at the hands of the Pittsburgh Public School Board.

At the time of this study, few comprehensive studies had been done on the subject of teacher discrimination for any major United States city. The studies that did exist focused on systems and situations which were not quite comparable to those which Blacks faced in Pittsburgh.

A number of existing articles on Black school teachers dealt with Southern settings and focused on teacher attitudes and training, on the reasons for their placement in certain subject areas, and on their displacement when Southern dual school systems were integrated. In Pittsburgh, however, as in other Northern cities, Blacks were employed in an essentially integrated system and the problem of teacher displacement was not as important.

Most studies of the experiences of Black teachers in Northern locales, such as Pennsylvania, Indiana and New York, focused mainly on Black students and the effects of the 1954 Supreme Court decision,

Brown vs. the Board of Education of Topeka, Kansas. In this landmark decision, the United States Supreme Court decreed that "separate but equal" educational systems were unconstitutional. The few articles which were concerned with Black teachers focused on what would happen to them in what were basically all-Black school systems. Although they concluded that Black teachers had been discriminated against, these studies did not present a detailed analysis of the kind and scope of discrimination, nor did they deal with the changing pattern of that discrimination.

David Tyack, for example, in his book *The One Best System*, indicates that in 1902, out of a total of 585 teachers in elementary schools in Indianapolis, the 53 who were Black were assigned to teach in "colored schools." He talks about the low number of Black teachers in urban schools in 1908 and describes Indiana's attempt to legislate against discrimination, based on race, in the hiring of teachers. Tyack concludes that Black teachers and administrators were discriminated against in virtually all public school systems.[6]

An article in *Integrated Education* concerned a report by the Pennsylvania Human Relations Commission which found that Chester, Pennsylvania, schools discriminated against Black teachers. This discrimination was accomplished by assigning every Black teacher and clerk to all-Black schools.[7] C.H. Thompson, in a 1953 article on school desegregation, dealt with what might happen to Black teachers once schools were integrated. He felt that most Black teachers would lose their jobs or be assigned to inferior schools.[8] Dwight W. Culver, in a 1954 article, talks about the desegregation of Indiana schools. He found that Black teachers were integrated at a very slow pace and that the Board of Education discriminated against Blacks by placing them in predominantly Black schools.[9]

In a 1963 study about California, C. Wilson Record cited a California State Department of Education report that stated that Blacks

---

6 David B. Tyack, *The One Best System—A History of American Urban Education* (Cambridge: Harvard University Press, 1974).

7 "The Chester Case," A report by the Pennsylvania Human Relations Commission, Integrated Education, 13 (1965), 15-25.

8 "Negro Teachers and Desegregation of Public Schools," editorial, *Journal of Negro Education* 22 (1953): 95-101.

9 Dwight W. Culver, "Racial Desegregation in Education in Indiana," *Journal of Negro Education*, 23 (1954): 296-302.

were employed in only 6% of the California school districts that had an integrated student population. Record said that the school boards explained their failure to hire Blacks by claiming that no qualified Blacks could be found. They further stated that if Blacks were hired, white teachers, students and parents would object.[10]

Neil Betten and Raymond A. Mohl focused on the development of racism in Gary, Indiana. The authors reported that Black teachers were discriminated against from 1906 to 1940 by a school system controlled by business leaders. In Gary, as in several other cities, Blacks were confined to a separate school system for many years.[11]

In sum, there was a great deal of information on Blacks and educational discrimination, but most of it was written about Black students, was focused on the Southern part of the United States, or was written about the period after 1954. The articles that did mention Black teachers in a Northern urban setting did not present a detailed, historical analysis of the discrimination faced by these Black teachers.

This study differed from most others in that it was a systematic analysis of the employment of Black Teachers and professionals in a Northern industrial city. It also differs in that this study made extensive use of oral history techniques. The study focused not only on the system of discrimination and the statistics involved, but also on the people behind the statistics who worked long and hard in securing equal employment opportunities for Blacks in the Pittsburgh school system. Equally importantly, this study explored the feelings of those early Black teachers in Pittsburgh. Through sharing their stories, this study told of the problems they faced and the victories they won.

---

10 C. Wilson Record, "School Board and Negro Teachers in California," *Integrated Education* 12 (1963): 22.
11 Neil Betten and Raymond A. Mohl, "The Evolution of Racism in an Industrial City, 1906-1940: A Case Study of Gary, Indiana," *Journal of Negro History* 59 (1974): 51-64

John M. Brewer *(2nd from right)*. **Graduation photograph with Igal Elam Spraggins, Dr. William Thomas Reed, Walter Pedro Newbern, and Harold L. Scott. John Brewer was a physical education teacher who was hired to run a summer program for children in an effort to curtail gang membership. – February 1947**

Leaders and participants in Hill District playground program, *back row from left:* **Michael Dadasovich, John Brewer Sr., Pomeroyal Fountain, Marion Staunton, John Morton;** *front row:* **Bobby Anderson, J. Morsee, Peggy Carter, Marvin Richter, Lois Roll, Eloise Clark, and Eugene Gelter – July 1941**

CHAPTER 1

The Wall of Discrimination

Introduction

Discrimination against Black teachers and professionals in the Pittsburgh Public School system can best be understood as one aspect of the general racial discrimination which Blacks faced, including employment, public accommodations, and housing. This chapter first traces the growth, migration and settlement patterns of Blacks who came to Pittsburgh during the late 19th and early 20th centuries. It then deals with the kinds of general racial discrimination Blacks faced in the Pittsburgh area.

Growth of the Black Population in Pittsburgh

As Table 1-1 shows, the growth of the Black population in Pittsburgh was steady. In the mid-1800s, when Pittsburgh set up its public school system, there were certainly enough Blacks for the Central Board of Education to consider the issue of Black education. Moreover, the Black population of Pittsburgh experienced even greater growth during the decades from 1880 to 1920. With over 50,000 Black residents in the city by 1930, certainly their number was significant enough that the city could not ignore the presence of its Black citizens. Blacks would have to be dealt with in housing, employment and public accommodations, as well as in education.

TABLE 1-1* **BLACK POPULATION GROWTH IN PITTSBURGH BY DECADE**	
YEAR	**POPULATION**
1840	823
1850	1,964
1860	1,149
1870	1,996
1880	4,077
1890	10,359
1900	21,355
1910	25,623
1920	37,725
1930	54,983
1940	62,216
1950	84,453

*Sources: U.S. Census Bureau;
Ann Wilmott, *Pittsburgh and the Blacks:
A Short History, 1780 to 1875* (unpublished dissertation,
Pennsylvania State University, 1975);
Peter Gottlieb, *Making Their Own Way: Southern Blacks
Migration to Pittsburgh, 1916-1930* (unpublished dissertation,
University of Pittsburgh, 1977)

Table 1-2 shows that most of the growth of the Pittsburgh population from 1915 to1929 came as a result of migration from the South, particularly Alabama and Georgia.

TABLE 1-2* PERCENTAGE OF BLACK PITTSBURGHERS BY DATE & STATE OF BIRTH			
STATE	1915-1919	1920-1924	1925-1929
Alabama	23.1	15.3	10.5
Georgia	18.4	17.9	10.8
Virginia	9.5	8.8	8.0
S. Carolina	5.6	9.7	8.1
N. Carolina	5.2	6.0	6.4
Mississippi	3.1	2.0	<1.0
Tennessee	2.9	2.5	1.9
Pennsylvania	2.7	2.0	3.6
Other	10.0	9.5	8.2

* Peter Gottlieb, *Making Their Own Way: Southern Blacks Migration to Pittsburgh, 1916-1930*, Unpublished doctoral dissertation, University of Pittsburgh, 1977, page 34.

Settlement Patterns

We have looked at the growth of the Black population and the origins of that growth. The next issue is where the migrants settled. Figure 1-1 is a map of Pittsburgh communities showing the various communities by name. For many years Blacks were segregated into certain specific areas. Pittsburgh, unlike many other Northern cities, did not develop one major Black ghetto. Rather, several sections of the city developed their own distinct Black ghettos. Almost from the beginning of Black migration to

Pittsburgh, there have been several sections of the city with substantial Black populations. Some of these communities shifted and changed, but there always remained several Black ghettos.

Ann Wilmoth says that in the nineteenth century Blacks in Pittsburgh lived in many areas of the city, but most lived in a few wards. The largest Black community was called Hayti and spanned the third, fourth and seventh wards. She also states that housing segregation, based on race, did not appear to be well defined.[12]

Abraham Epstein indicates that, in 1918, there were several Black communities:

- The Hill and upper Wylie and Bedford Avenues;
- Lawrenceville around Penn Avenue between 34th and 28th streets;
- The North Side around Beaver Avenue and Fulton;
- East Liberty in the vicinity of Mignonette and Shakespeare Streets;
- Downtown Pittsburgh on Second Avenue and Ross Street at Water Street.

Figure 1-1. The Study Area: Communities of Pittsburgh

Epstein indicates that areas previously designated for Blacks had long since been overcrowded, and new settlements of Blacks were

---

12 Ann G. Wilmoth, *Pittsburgh and the Blacks: A Short History, 1780 – 1875*, Unpublished doctoral dissertation, Pennsylvania State University, 1975, pages 1, 24.

formed in hollows and ravines on hillsides by the rivers and by railroads and mills.[13]

Joe T. Darden, in his book on residential segregation in Pittsburgh, states that from 1930 to 1970 at least two thirds of the Black population of Pittsburgh was concentrated in three areas: the Hill, Homewood-Brushton, and East Liberty. According to Darden, by 1930 Blacks lived in the following areas (Figure 1-1):

- the South Side: Broadhead, Chicken Hill, Beechview, Beltzhoover;
- the North Side: Woods Run, Chateau, Manchester, Lower North Side, Perry South, parts of the upper North Side
- the East End: part of Stanton Heights, Bloomfield, East Liberty, Larimer, Lincoln, Shadyside, Homewood-Brushton
- the City Center Pittsburgh: the lower Hill, middle Hill, upper Hill, the Strip, Polish Hill, Herron Hill, Soho, Hazelwood. [14]

While some of these areas would change over the next forty years, the fact remains that there continued to be several Black communities separated by rivers, hills, time and distance.

This diversification of the Black community rather than the establishment of one or even two Black communities became very important as Blacks attempted to deal with the problems they faced in Pittsburgh. Each separate district developed stereotyped ideas about the Black inhabitants in the other areas. The author recalls quite vividly the shock expressed by his mother when he offhandedly said he was dating a young lady from the North Side. His mother stated that he should be careful, because "those people" on the North Side were very violent. At the same time, the young lady's mother was warning her about dating a person from the Hill, because "those people" were violent. Often when youngsters from one Black area visited another Black area, physical violence would occur as a result of territorial infringements. Given all these factors it is no wonder that even during the height of the

---

13 Abraham Epstein, *The Negro Migrant in Pittsburgh* (Pittsburgh: School of Economics, University of Pittsburgh, 1918), 8, 29, 16.
14 Joe T. Darden, *Afro-Americans in Pittsburgh: The Residential Segregation of a People* (Lexington, Mass.: D.C. Heath and Company, 1973), 7.

civil rights movement it was difficult for Blacks to mount a concerted, organized effort. This inability to come together as a common group is a very important factor in explaining why the Pittsburgh Board of Public Education was able to avoid hiring Blacks much longer than school systems in other cities.

Relations with Other Ethnic Groups

When Blacks migrated to Pittsburgh they had to compete with a variety of ethnic groups including Italians, Irish, Poles and other Europeans. How did they get along with these groups? According to Ann Wilmoth, they got along pretty well in the 19th century. While Philadelphia experienced many race riots during the ante-bellum period, Pittsburgh survived the period with relatively few disturbances. Wilmoth further indicates that some racial violence did occur in Pittsburgh but not to the same extent as in some other cities.[15]

I asked several of the individuals I interviewed how they viewed relationships between Blacks and other ethnic groups in the more recent period. Despite stories in various newspapers about racial friction, the consensus was that Blacks and members of ethnic groups got along very well. Many spoke in glowing terms of the "old days" in the lower Hill where ethnic groups lived and worked together in harmony. The author's father worked in this area as a butcher in a shop owned by a Jewish family. Each Christmas he would take his children to Logan Street to buy their Christmas tree from an Italian man who played Christmas songs on a guitar. A young white woman told the author that her mother often spent long hours talking with old friends about how well everyone got along in those earlier times in the Lower Hill. Most of the people interviewed for this study expressed great sorrow that the Logan Street area was destroyed to make way for Urban Renewal. Actually those "old days" were not so long ago given that the Urban renewal projects that decimated this area were completed in the late 1950s.

Perhaps most of the racial problems occurred as a result of interaction with whites who did not live in close proximity to Blacks. It appears that Blacks and other ethnic groups got along well because they

---

15 Wilmoth, page 22.

shared common problems and because that close proximity allowed them to see one another as human beings and not as enemies.

Other Kinds of Discrimination

In most cases the housing for Black migrants was woefully inadequate. Some buildings had already been declared unfit for human habitation; some had been converted from chicken stores and horse stables; most were overcrowded. Many Blacks were forced to pay high rents for crowded apartments or small homes.[16]

While a great deal of information was not available on housing for Blacks in the 19th century, that which was available indicates that Blacks were for the most part relegated to housing that was less suitable than that available for whites.[17]

Speaking of housing for Blacks in 20th century Pittsburgh, Epstein states that attics, cellars, storefronts, basements, churches, sheds, and warehouses were used to house Black migrants and that the majority of Blacks living in Pittsburgh converted their homes into boarding houses. He further indicates that:

> Of men without families 22 out of 300 had single bedrooms, 25% lived four in a room, 25% with more than four in a room, 37% slept in separate beds, 50% in beds with two people, and 13% in beds with three or more in a bed ...

> In many cases, houses in which these rooms are located are dilapidated dwellings with the paper torn off, the plaster sagging from the naked lath, the windows broken, the ceiling low and damp, and the whole room dark, stuffy and unsanitary.

> In the more crowded sections, beds are rented on a double shift basis. Men who work at night sleep during the day in beds vacated by day workers.[18]

16 Ralph and Ruby Proctor and Harry and Bee Latimer in discussions with author, 1970-1974.
17 James Dean and John and Martha Blanding in discussions with author, 1970-1973.
18 Epstein, pages 8, 18.

Epstein also says that few of the dwellings rented to Blacks had toilets or water located inside. Eighty-one of the total of 139 houses he studied had water inside the house. Fifty-eight of the houses got water from hydrants located in the yard or on the street or they got water from neighbors. Only 34 had inside toilets. Few of the dwellings had gas stoves. Coal and wood were used for cooking and heating. This forced residents to cook on red-hot stoves even during the hottest times of the year. Many Black residents complained that housing conditions in Pittsburgh were far worse than those they had left in the South.

Employment discrimination was rampant in almost every field. In 19th century Pittsburgh, most Blacks worked in unskilled jobs such as common laborers, seamen, coachmen, waiters, whitewashers, servants, barbers, house-keepers and washerwomen.[19] Between 1910 and 1930, the majority of Black women worked in domestic and personal service jobs such as barbers, hairdressers, cleaners, servants, and untrained nurses. During that same time Black men labored either in the domestic service or in the manufacturing field.[20]

Better jobs were reserved for whites. Blacks were forced to take menial jobs such as domestic workers, janitors, chauffeurs, porters, ditch diggers, hod carriers and waiters. Often even those jobs were closed to Blacks. For the most part, Blacks received less money than whites for performing the same tasks. As Harry Lattimer, a longtime Hill resident, said, "You didn't worry about being promoted or getting a raise; you worried about keeping the job you had."[21] Blacks were encouraged to enter trade schools, while at the same time trade unions refused to accept Black members. Until 1947 there were no Blacks employed in downtown department stores.

As reported in different issues of *The Pittsburgh Courier*, there were numerous racial incidents in the public school system, ranging from the reading of "pickaninny" stories to white students portraying unflattering Black characters in plays. Black students were discouraged from preparing for professions by teachers and counselors. Universities discriminated against Blacks in admission and hiring. Hospitals

---

19 Wilmoth, page 9.
20 Gottlieb, pages 125, 132.
21 Harry Latimer in discussion with author, 1974.

refused to train Blacks as nurses. Hospitals not only discriminated in their training, they also segregated patients by race and were repeatedly accused of treating Blacks poorly. Many hospitals during the time refused to accept Black physicians on their staffs.[22]

There was constant friction between the Black community and the Police Department. There were repeated articles in *The Pittsburgh Courier* about Blacks being shot to death by police. Black citizens accused the police of harassment. In addition, the Police Department was accused of not hiring enough Black police and of not promoting those already hired.

Blacks were limited as to where they could go for entertainment, food, or lodgings. They were not admitted to most white-owned hotels, refused service in many white- owned bars and restaurants, refused admission to some theaters and forced to sit in the upper balcony in others. They were initially not allowed in swimming pools throughout the area, and when they did attempt to swim they were often beaten by whites while the police looked on.[23]

It is evident, then, that while conditions were somewhat better in Pittsburgh than in the South, this was not the "promised land" by any means. Blacks made a little more money and enjoyed a bit more freedom, but discrimination was the rule rather than the exception.

Interviews reveal that discrimination was not an unchanging phenomenon as one might expect from reading the newspaper accounts alone. There was change. Harry Latimer says that the pattern of discrimination changed from the time he was a boy. When he was a youngster, discrimination was very subtle; but when he returned from the service in the 1940s, racism had become more blatant. Examination of *The Pittsburgh Courier* supports his feelings in that there were more reported incidents of discrimination in 1945 and 1946. The higher number of reported incidents in those years might also have something to do with Blacks being more likely to report such incidents or simply being more sensitive to discrimination. It might also express the unwillingness of people who had been involved in a war to settle for the same kind of treatment they had experienced before. In light of

---

22 Multiple issues of *The Pittsburgh Courier*, 1927-1973.
23 Herb Wilkerson and Alma Fox in discussion with the author, 1975

this, it is curious that most of the subjects of my interviews felt that, in general, race relations were "pretty good."

The data suggest that if a person lived and worked and sought entertainment in the Hill or other areas where there was a high concentration of Blacks, the chances of being discriminated against were considerably reduced. If, however, one went to parts of the East End, Homewood-Brushton, Oakland, Shadyside, or downtown Pittsburgh, there was a very good chance of encountering discrimination. Harry Latimer said that Oakland, the location of the University of Pittsburgh, was the most prejudiced section of town.[24] It is a matter of record that the NAACP was still actively involved in breaking down racial barriers in housing, education and public accommodations in Oakland as late as the middle of the 1960s. Newspaper accounts verify that there were sections of Pittsburgh where Blacks were more likely to be discriminated against.[25]

Were conditions better here in the North for Blacks? Again, my interviewees said in general they were, but John Blanding, who had lived in the Hill since the 1930s, said that he heard more whites use the word "nigger" here in the North than he had ever heard in the South.[26] Roosevelt Holly, who worked in Southern hotels, said that there were jobs Blacks could get in the South that they could not get in Pittsburgh. He had worked as a bellhop in the South and had applied for the same position at some of the hotels in Pittsburgh. He was informed that Pittsburgh hotels did not employ Blacks in that capacity.[27] So, while things were better for Blacks in some situations, it seems clear that the North was not better for Blacks in every respect.

While the picture of employment was very bad in 1900, it did change as time passed. Though initially there were no Blacks in high positions in the legal system, a Black judge was appointed in 1950. From 1900 to the late 1940s, no Blacks worked as clerks in downtown department stores, but by the end of the 1940s they were being hired. The Pittsburgh Pirates baseball team initially did not hire Blacks; by 1941 three Blacks were allowed to try out for the team. The Pittsburgh Railway Company made no excuses about not hiring Blacks. They

24 Harry Latimer in discussion with the author, 1974.
25 Multiple issues of *The Pittsburgh Courier*, 1927-1973.
26 John Blanding in discussion with author, 1974.
27 Roosevelt Holly in discussion with author, 1973.

simply said that it was "not their policy." The first Black bus driver was hired in 1946.

Blacks were discriminated against in public accommodations, though each year brought a few more places Blacks could go to. By 1950, Kennywood Park swimming pool was opened to Blacks by a court order. Black life guards were hired at pools and eventually most public pools were opened to Blacks, though some would remain segregated until well into the 1960s.

Most businesses in the Hill in the early 20th century belonged to whites, but there were more Black businesses in the area from 1930 to 1950 than there are at the time of this study. Relations between Blacks and the Police Department remained tense and strained during this entire period. Wilmoth, in speaking about racial discrimination in Pittsburgh, stated that while no evidence suggested that Pittsburgh had a formal Black code, discrimination did exist. Blacks had separate sections in courts and theatres, attended segregated schools, worshipped in their own churches and were buried in segregated cemeteries.[28]

The pattern of racism and discrimination was changing and flexible, sometimes easily recognized and at other times well hidden. It is a complicated system about which few gross generalizations can safely be made, but it did change over time. Public accommodations were largely closed to Blacks in the early part of the century, but by the late 1960s were open for the most part. However, even at the time of this study, Blacks were still not welcome in some areas, especially in some communities outside the central city.

Housing patterns also changed and Blacks enjoyed easier access to white communities. Still in the late 1970s Blacks in the city of Pittsburgh could not yet be certain that if they answered a housing related ad in *The Pittsburgh Press* or *The Pittsburgh Post-Gazette*, they would not encounter discrimination when attempting to buy or rent an apartment or house. The range of employment opportunities had improved since the early 1900s. Blacks are no longer relegated to service jobs or as James Dean, who had lived in various Black areas since coming to Pittsburgh in the early 1930s, put it, "driving the rich man's carriage."[29]

---

28 Wilmoth, pages 25, 29.
29 James Dean in discussion with author, 1972.

The education of Blacks was another area that had undergone change. At first Blacks were confined to an all-Black system and then discriminated against in an integrated one. The Pittsburgh Board of Education had not yet come up with an integration plan that is acceptable to the Black community or Federal and State authorities.

Black teachers had been subjected to a constantly changing pattern of discrimination in public, private, elementary, secondary and higher educational facilities. In the next few chapters we will examine the plight and progress of Black teachers in the Pittsburgh Public School system.

CHAPTER 2

The First Black Teachers in Pittsburgh

Introduction

This chapter is concerned with the first Black teachers hired to teach public school in Pittsburgh, Pennsylvania. It begins with an examination of the separate school system set up by the Central School Board in response to demands by Blacks that their children be provided with a public education. This Central School Board would also control the Education of Blacks by providing a "Colored School Committee" consisting of one member from each Ward School District to administer the "colored school." This chapter traces the development of that separate school system from its inception to its closing in 1881. It will detail the efforts of the Black community to exercise some control over the affairs of the "colored schools." The Central Board, again in response to Black pressure, formed an informal committee of Black citizens to offer advice on the separate school system. This committee was dissolved when the Blacks took their task seriously and put too much pressure on the Board.

Finally, this chapter deals with the Black teachers who were hired to teach in the "colored schools." It details how Black teachers were no longer hired once Black students were allowed to attend an integrated school system.

While Pittsburgh Blacks struggled to get a few Black teachers hired as part of the faculty in the integrated system, other cities had already begun to hire Black teachers even though most of them were teaching in all-Black schools. Obviously Pittsburgh was lagging behind other cities in the hiring of Black teachers. The question is why did Pittsburgh fail to hire Black teachers as soon as other cities did? There are several possible answers: the lack of unity and militancy on the part of Blacks; the scattered nature of the Black community; the indifference of the School Board.

The Separate School System in Pittsburgh

The Pennsylvania State Temporary Commission on Urban Colored Population, charged with the task of studying the status of Pennsylvania Blacks, in 1943 stated, "The Continental Congress considered it useless to educate Negroes and for a long time in Pennsylvania it was a felony for a Negro 'to be caught with a book in his hands'."[1]

The Acts of 1802 and 1804, which provided free education for poor children, did not mention the Negro. Although free schools actually came later, Blacks were excluded. It was assumed that Blacks would not attend school with Whites, but it seemed that nothing could be done to provide any sort of public education for Pennsylvania's Black students. Black citizens, realizing that there were no plans to include their children in the public school system in Pittsburgh, began to make plans to educate their own children.

In 1818, the first school for Black children in Pittsburgh was opened. It failed for lack of support or funds. In 1832, Blacks met in the African Methodist Episcopal Church to organize the Pittsburgh African Educational Society and to elect officers of the organization. The officers included the leading figures of the Black community— John B. Vashon, Louis Woodson, and A.O. Lewis. The organization opened one school, but it too soon failed because of lack of funds.[2]

By 1835, Pittsburgh had opened four free public schools. No Blacks were allowed to attend and all the instructors were White. The four schools were located in what were called the West Ward, the South Ward, the East Ward, and the North Ward of Pittsburgh. On December 18, 1835, Blacks in Pittsburgh sent the following letter to the Director of the Second Ward (or South School District) School:

---

1   "Report of the Pennsylvania State Temporary Commission on Urban Colored Population," (Harrisburg, January 1943), page 381.

2   "Report of the Pennsylvania State Temporary Commission on Urban Colored Population," (Harrisburg, January 1943), page 381.

FIGURE 2-1*

To the Directors of the Public Schools of the City of Pittsburgh

We the colored citizens whose names are hereunto subscribed do sincerely petition to them as we paid tax for the said schools and as yet receive no benefit therefrom and as we are not the most part able to school our children although we have a house and children. Numbers cannot come on account of not being able to pay the teacher. Therefore we do sincerely hope that the authority in the City be please to let the different wards of our city be kept at our house in First Street between Wood and Smithfield Street.

> Yours most humbly praying,
> Thomas Norris
> Samuel Johnson
> A.O. Lewis
> George Gardner

*Erasmus Wilson, ed., *Standard History of Pittsburgh, Pennsylvania* (Chicago: H.R. Cornell § Company, 1898), page 514.

Significantly, Blacks were not then asking for admission to the White schools, but instead were asking the Central Board of Education to allow Blacks from all Wards to attend the school operated by Blacks and that the Board pay the teacher. This very mild request was ignored.

In January 1837, Blacks once again attempted to get the Central Board of Education to respond to the issue of educating Black youngsters. The following letter was sent to the Directors of the School Board.

FIGURE 2-2*

To the School Directors of the City of Pittsburgh

Gentlemen:

The undersigned believe that the laws of this state providing for the education of the children of the poor classes of her population at public expense contemplate no distinction between white and colored children. They therefore respectfully ask whether colored children will be received into the schools under your care and if not whether other schools exclusively for their benefit will be established or whether any appropriations of money will be made for the support of such schools for colored children as are now in existence and which are now sustained chiefly if not entirely by tuition.

(Signed)
Charles Avery
Samuel Church
Alex Laughlin

*William Daniel McCoy, "History of Pittsburgh Public Schools to 1942," unpublished notes of October 1959, Vol. II, 174 (Hillman Library, University of Pittsburgh).

Finally, the Board relented to the pressure from Blacks and established a school for Black children. The first school, opened in 1837, was housed in the Baptist Church on Robinson Street. Another was opened in 1838, and was located in a small church in Litenberger Alley. The two Black schools spent the next few years being moved around the city. Records are very scarce on their movements, but as nearly as can be figured, one or the other occupied the following locations at various times:

      1844   Sherman Avenue, in a Baptist church
      1846   Avery Street
      1848   Wylie Avenue A.M.E. Church in the lower basement

1848   Bethel A.M.E. Church on Arthur Street at some point in a church called Temperance Ark

1855   Wesleyan Methodist Church on Wylie Avenue, in the basement

1859   Universal Chapel in the 2nd Ward

In 1867 both schools were combined into the newly constructed Miller Street School building, which was erected specifically for use by Black students.

While the Pittsburgh "colored schools" were being bounced around the city, the State government acted to "solve" the problem of what to do with Black students. In 1854, Act #610, Section 24, required all districts to set up separate schools for Blacks. The Act said, "Districts are hereby authorized and required to establish separate schools for Negro and Mulatto children." This law remained in effect until 1881, when separate schools were abolished.

An examination of the hand-written minutes of the Central Board of Education revealed numerous entries having to do with the education of Black students.

> On March 27, 1855, a special meeting of the Central Board of Education was called in order that the Board might take action on the colored school. The entry on page 5 for that date reads, "the colored school will be opened April 1st and continued open until such time as the Board might otherwise order and that C. Sackett be employed to teach at the rate of $500 per year."

> On April 10, 1855, the Board minutes indicate that the rear basement room of the Wesleyan Methodist Church on Wiley Street had been rented for the "colored school" at the rate of $100 per year from the first of April 1855.

> On January 21, 1856, the Board passed a resolution hiring Miss Susan P. Smith as an assistant teacher in the "colored school" as of February 1, 1856.

The entry for October 13, 1857 indicates that "some prominent colored citizens" suggested the name of C.B. Vashon as a "competent colored teacher" who could teach in the separate school system.

As of April 9, 1867, the Board started serious work on setting up a separate building to house the Black students. It was announced that a lot for erecting the "colored school" had been purchased on Miller Street in the Hill District. For some time after the opening of the Miller Street School, or as it was called, the "colored school," members of the Central Board of Education complained that the school was a costly financial drain. As a result of this feeling, at the April 14, 1874, meeting the Board's legislative committee was instructed to prepare and forward to Harrisburg a bill repealing the act requiring separate schools for colored children. In 1881, the State did repeal this law and the Miller Street School was closed. The Black students were then sent to Ward schools in the areas of their residence.

The popular fiction in the City of Pittsburgh is that the first Black person ever to teach in the Pittsburgh Public School system was hired in 1937. The research for this project indicates that this is not so. While the records are, at best, very sketchy and incomplete, it is evident that some "known" Blacks were teaching in the so-called "colored schools." The term "known" Blacks is used because, at best, one can only guess at the date for the hiring of the first Black teacher, since all Blacks were not easily identifiable. Since the beginning of interracial sexual encounters in the days of slavery, some Blacks have crossed unnoticed into the "White" world.

Even though the evidence is not complete, it can be said with some certainty that Blacks taught in the Pittsburgh Public School system before the 20th century. The first Black to teach in the Pittsburgh system was John M. Templeton in 1837.[3]

No records were located to indicate who the teachers in the "colored schools" were from 1837 to 1855. However, in 1855, a Mr. C. Sackett was hired as a teacher. Unfortunately, no mention was made of his race.

---

3   William Daniel McCoy, "History of Pittsburgh Public Schools to 1942," unpublished notes of October 1959, Vol. II, 174 (University of Pittsburgh, Hillman Library), page 175.

In 1857, at the request of Black citizens, Mr. G.B. Vashon, a leading figure in the Black community, was hired to teach in the "colored school." While Mr. C. Sackett was the head teacher at the school, a Ms. Susan P. Smith was hired as a teaching assistant. In the July 18, 1859 minutes of the Board is the following entry on page 246, "Mr. George B. Vashon was elected principal of the colored school and Mrs. Susan P. Vashon was elected assistant teacher."

On May 8, 1860, Mrs. Emily Burr was hired as an assistant teacher for the Black school; again, there is no mention of race. On July 12, 1864, Mr. C. Sackett was reelected to the "colored school." No mention was made on either date as to what happened to Mr. or Mrs. Vashon.

Blacks again pressed for the hiring of a Black teacher and on July 23, 1867, the Board minutes indicate that a "committee of colored citizens"—consisting of A.F. Billows, John W. Little and James W. Owens—pushed for the appointment of a Black man by the name of Jacob B. Taylor. He was elected. At the same time the Board elected Mr. Taylor to his teaching position, they elected two women to positions of assistant teachers, but there was no mention of race. Mr. David W. Atwood was elected to the head position at the Black school on November 10, 1868, to replace Mr. Taylor, who had resigned.

A committee of Blacks voiced dissatisfaction with Mr. Atwood and pressed for the re-appointment of Mr. Taylor. The Committee for Colored Schools overruled their objections.

On November 9, 1869, Black citizens protested the Board's efforts to close Miller School. They asked for the organization of other Black schools in different parts of the city, protested the appointment of another white woman as teacher, asked the Board to hire a Black person and, finally, demanded the removal of the Chairman of the Colored School Committee and the appointment of someone more sympathetic to Blacks. On January 11, 1870, Mrs. Ella Connelly and Mrs. Maria Baker were hired to replace Mrs. Ware and Mrs. Burr. Unfortunately, one is again left to guess at the race of Mrs. Connelly and Mrs. Baker.

On August 9, 1870, Blacks again petitioned the Board for the appointment of colored teachers, and said that they had several applicants who were ready to take their teacher's examinations. On September 13, 1870, however, the Board defiantly elected D.M.

Atwood as Principal and Mr. F.A. Harris, Mrs. S.H. Barker, and Mrs. K.P. Hartman as teachers, over the objections of Black citizens.

Others were elected to the "colored schools" at various times, but no further mention was made of race. They were:

Kate M. Harker	February 14, 1870
F.R.H. Johnson	August 13, 1872
Jennie McClure	August 13, 1872
Fannie Hanes	March 11, 1873
T.R. Johnson	August 12, 1873
Harriet Saunder	August 12, 1873
Mrs. Harris	August 12, 1873
Mrs. Kate Kelly	October 12, 1875

While one cannot say how many Black teachers there were since the beginning of the Pittsburgh Public School system, it can definitely be stated that the Central Board of Education did employ some Blacks beginning in 1837 (Table 2-1).

TABLE 2-1		
BLACK TEACHERS IN "COLORED" SCHOOLS		
1837	John M. Templeton	Principal & Teacher
1859	George B. Vashon	Principal & Teacher
1867	Jacob B. Taylor	Principal & Teacher
Unknown	Martin Delaney	Principal & Teacher

All of them were employed in the "colored schools." No "known" Black teachers were employed in the other schools, which contained all White students. The numbers and who these Black teachers were are not as important as the fact that Blacks were employed by the Central Board of Education as teachers before the 20th century.

Another interesting fact presents itself in the pages of the minutes of the Central Board of Education—those teachers who taught in the "colored schools" were paid less than their counterparts in the all-White schools, at least for many of the operational years of the separate school system. Salaries in the two school systems are presented in Table 2-2. It was not until after 1867 that the salaries of teachers and principals were equalized, whether they taught in the colored or white schools.

		SCHOOL	
YEAR	**JOB CLASSIFICATION**	**COLORED**	**WHITE**
1856	Principal	$500	$900
	Assistant Teacher	$250	$400-500
1859	Principal	$600	$900
	Assistant Teacher	$250	$400-500
1862	Principal	$550	$800
	Assistant Teacher	$220	$320+
1864	Principal	$700	$950
	Assistant Teacher	$300	$300
1866	Principal	$1,000	$1,350

TABLE 2-2
SALARY COMPARISON BY YEAR, JOB CLASSIFICATION, & SCHOOL

While the Blacks did pressure the Central Board of Education for the hiring of Black teachers, there is no evidence of any organized resistance from Blacks to the concept of separate schools. In fact, it seems that Blacks were more concerned about opening up additional separate schools for Blacks so that children from other parts of the city would not have to travel to the Miller Street School. When, in the latter part of the nineteenth century, the Board tried to abandon the colored school because of its cost, Blacks strongly objected. They accepted the idea of a separate school system, whether on the basis of racial pride or the fear that if the Board closed the colored school free education for Black children would come to an end is not clear. Blacks may also have opposed this move because they knew that the Board would not hire Black teachers to teach in the other schools. What is known is that the Central Board of Education was pressuring the state legislature to abolish separate schools for Blacks so that the Miller School building could be sold.[4]

---

4   McCoy, pages 181-185.

The Miller Street School was closed in 1881. The Black students were distributed among the Ward schools and are not mentioned again in Board of Education minutes. After the colored school was closed, so did the book close on employment of Black teachers. According to its own statistics and the words of Blacks and Whites alike, no "known" Blacks would be hired to teach in the Pittsburgh Public School system on a full-time basis until 1937.

The Intervening Years

From the time the "colored school" was closed in 1881 until 1937, no Black teachers were hired by the Pittsburgh Public School system on a full-time basis. The minutes of the Central Board of Education do not again mention contacts with Black groups on the hiring of Black teachers. In fact, no mention of Blacks at all can be found in any of the remaining minutes books which continue until June 10, 1890.

In 1911, the Central Board of Education became the Pittsburgh Board of Public Education. The same absence of virtually any mention of Blacks is also evident upon examining published minutes of the Board of Education from 1911 to 1937. It was as if the Board of Education had decided that the issue no longer existed. It is evident that the Board did not discuss the issue at meetings or simply did not include those discussions in the minutes.

While the Pittsburgh Board of Education acted as if no problems existed relative to the employment of Black teachers, the situation was changing elsewhere in the North. Cities such as Gary, Cleveland, Philadelphia, Washington, D.C., and Indianapolis had begun to employ Black teachers in the 19th century and Black Pittsburghers were upset that the Pittsburgh School Board would not hire Blacks.

In 1914, Robert L. Vann, editor of the *Pittsburgh Courier*, began a campaign to get Black teachers employed in the city of Pittsburgh. In an editorial he said:

> That Cleveland should find employment for thirty
> Negro school teachers in the city schools argues
> emphatically that there is a better civic order in the
> Forest City than we enjoy here. The effort and energy

employed in securing the representation the Negroes enjoy in Cleveland must be employed here.

What we need is a concerted effort in the proper direction, with the least possible suspicion that someone wants separate schools. We are satisfied with the schools, our objection is to the present all-white personnel of the teachers.[5]

In his master's thesis, James H. Brewer quotes Vann as having advocated Black teachers for Black students during the early years of schooling.[6] Andrew Buni, in his book <u>Robert L. Vann of the Pittsburgh Courier</u>, talks further about Vann's attitude towards the issue in 1914:

When a young Black woman made known her hope of being a teacher in Pittsburgh, he devoted two long editorials to the topic. 'The Negro population must to a man stand behind this young woman ... *The Courier* admonishes every man and woman to demand that this right be extended.' In April, Vann noted the 'precarious condition of our school facilities ... we need MIXED SCHOOLS AND MIXED TEACHERS.' Vann had once given a long speech on the need for young Blacks to have Black teachers to identify with: In that editorial Vann had said that Black children need Black teachers because Black teachers best exhibited the sympathy, patience, interest and love that Black students needed.[7]

Richard F. Jones, one of the early Black attorneys, feels that one problem facing Blacks in their early efforts to secure positions for Black teachers in Pittsburgh was the division in the Black community as to whether the schools should be integrated or segregated. One group felt that the only hope for Black employment was in a separate system

---

5 McCoy, page 179.
6 James H. Brewer, *Robert L. Vann and The Pittsburgh Courier*, unpublished Master's thesis (University of Pittsburgh, 1941), page 60.
7 Brewer, page 62.

with all-Black faculties. Another group felt that Blacks should press for mixed schools and mixed faculties. Attorney Jones was in the latter category.[8]

It is difficult at this time to accurately identify the members of each group. While conducting the interviews, the author found much disagreement as to who belonged to the "separatist" group and who belonged to the "integrationists." In fact, some people were identified as having been members of both groups. It does seem, however, that at least some of the members of the separatist group wanted the separate school system because they felt that this was the only way Blacks were going to be employed in the public school system. It is also clear that some of the members of this group included people who had come from areas where separate Black school systems already existed. They felt that this could be a good answer for Pittsburgh's problems as well. There do not seem to be such clearly definable characteristics about the integrationist group, except that they seemed to have been long-term residents of the area.

Speaking further on the issue of segregated versus integrated schools, Jones told the author: "All the Blacks involved (among the separatists) at first were native southerners. All these had reached the conclusion that Blacks would have to accept separate schools." Jones felt this would be a mistake because "no intellectual effort had been made by Pittsburgh Negroes to obtain employment in mixed schools, and we should not accept less."

Jones felt that the reason Blacks were ready to accept separate schools was because Philadelphia had a *de facto* segregated school system and there were "lots of Black teachers." Jones continues, "They were ready to consummate such a deal for Pittsburgh, and I was very fearful and afraid that the separate school system would come about. I had become a lawyer to become independent, and not have to live in mental or physical slavery."[9] Speaking about attempts to convince the local School Board to hire Blacks, Jones said to others involved in the struggle, "We don't need to bow and scrape to the city. The discrimination is against the law--our approach must be public."

---

8   Andrew Bunik, *Robert L. Vann of The Pittsburgh Courier* (Pittsburgh: University of Pittsburgh Press, 1974), 67.

9   Richard Jones in discussion with the author, 1975.

When asked about the public's attitude toward the issue, Jones indicated that there was a general failure to recognize how many competent Blacks there were in Pittsburgh who could teach in the public school system. Few people were aware of the number of qualified Black teachers who had left Pittsburgh to find teaching positions elsewhere. The average person took it for granted that there were no qualified Blacks, and so they took the lack of Blacks in the school system as a reflection of that. People simply accepted the situation. Those who did not were ready to accept a separate school system.

One of the issues discussed by those involved in the efforts to secure Black teaching positions was the fact that a large portion of the Pittsburgh student population was Black, thus proving the need for Black teachers. Statistics as to the yearly growth of that Black population are sketchy. Table 2-3 presents a few of the available pieces of information relative to the Black student population.

TABLE 2-3
PARTIAL LIST OF BLACK STUDENTS IN PITTSBURGH PUBLIC SCHOOLS IN EARLY 20TH CENTURY

YEAR	APPROXIMATE # OF BLACK STUDENTS
1908	2,792 elementary school children*
1915	4,083 of 102,572 between the ages of 6 and 16**
1928	11,533***

*Richard Jones, 1975.
**David B. Tyack, *The One Best System – A History of American Urban Education* (Cambridge: Harvard University Press, 1974), page 117.
***James H. Brewer, page 61.

Table 2-4 shows that by 1928 Black students constituted a substantial proportion of the student population in many schools. This table shows that Black students were in the majority in at least five of the schools in the sample. Even in the face of this evidence of a large Black student population, the Board of Education refused to hire Black teachers.

TABLE 2-4*
BLACK STUDENT ENROLLMENT IN SELECTED PITTSBURGH PUBLIC ELEMENTARY SCHOOLS IN 1928**

SCHOOL	ENROLLMENT		
	TOTAL	# BLACK	% BLACK
Baxter	374	64	17
Crowley	887	151	17
Franklin	869	352	40.5
Garfield	639	101	16
Letsche	552	241	44
Lincoln	976	321	33
Linden	535	321	60
Madison	764	115	15
Manchester	1,658	218	13
Miller	821	161	20
Minersville	571	245	43
Penn	599	218	36
Rose	717	425	60
Shakespeare	390	102	26
Soho	824	253	31
Somers	314	219	70
Springfield	335	180	54
Thaddeus Stevens	364	63	17
Stevenson	23	8	35
Watt	1,055	904	86

*Untitled report, NAACP files, Archives of an Industrial Society,
Hillman Library, University of Pittsburgh.
**There were approximately 86 other elementary schools having no Black students.

In answering charges of racial discrimination, the Board of Education countered by saying that they could find no "qualified" Black graduates to teach in the public school system.[10] The Board insisted

---

10 "A Study of the Educational Department of the Pittsburgh Public Schools," Pittsburgh Board of Public Education, 1928, page 212.

upon perpetuating this official fiction even though it had graduated some Blacks from its own training school and Blacks were graduating from other colleges and universities throughout Pennsylvania and in Pittsburgh.

The author decided to examine copies of the University of Pittsburgh yearbook, *The Owl*, to see if the Board's contention of "no qualified Blacks" was true. Each available yearbook from 1907 to 1937 was examined to see how many Blacks had been graduated from the University of Pittsburgh. Photos of graduates from the College of Arts and Sciences and the School of Education were examined, since these were the areas from which teachers were likely to be drawn. If there were Blacks being graduated from Pitt in these areas, it is then certain that the Board of Education did, in fact, have a pool of "qualified" Blacks from which to choose. This visual method of examination underestimates the number of qualified Blacks since some Blacks who were not easily identifiable may not have been counted. This method shows that prior to 1937 at least fourteen Blacks had graduated from the University of Pittsburgh School of Education and another 34 had graduated from the College of Arts and Sciences.

YEAR	ARTS & SCIENCES	EDUCATION	TOTAL
TABLE 2-5* **PARTIAL LIST OF BLACK GRADUATES UNIVERSITY OF PITTSBURGH 1907-1937**			
1907	2		2
1908			0
1909			0
1910	1		1
1911			0
1912	1		1
1913			0
1914	1		1
1916		1	1
1921	1	1	2
1924			0
1925			0
1926	3	1	4
1927	1	2	3
1928	5	2	7
1929	2	2	4
1930	2	1	3
1931	8	2	10
1932	3	1	4
1933	1	1	2
1934	1		1
1935	1		1
1936	1		1
1937	2	3	5

The Owl, University of Pittsburgh Yearbooks, 1907-1921, 1924-1937.

From oral accounts the author gathered through interviews, we can learn something of what was happening to these graduates.[11]

---

11 Dates of interviews listed in the Information Sources under "Oral Interviews."

Frank Bolden, a Pitt graduate in 1937, went into journalism after being told by the Director of Personnel at the Board, "It's too bad you're not white. I'd hire you immediately." Mr. Bolden said, "If you wanted to teach school on any level and you were Black, you left Pittsburgh. If you didn't want to leave Pittsburgh, you didn't teach." He further indicated that many Blacks did not even attempt to apply for teaching positions in Pittsburgh because "they knew it would be a useless effort."

Attorney Richard Jones said that Dr. Davidson, Superintendent of the Board of Education, would attempt to get jobs in Indianapolis or Washington, D.C., for those Pittsburgh Blacks who insisted upon being employed by the Pittsburgh Board of Education.

Helen Miller Morrison related how, when she and her father went to see Dr. Davidson at the Board, he offered to try to get her a job in Indianapolis. Mrs. Morrison stated that Davidson showed them a letter from a friend of his who was the superintendent for the public schools in Indianapolis. One part of the letter said, "We take care of our colored girls, why don't you take care of yours?"

Georgine Pearce Brown indicated that her sister had gone to teach in Washington, D.C., because she could not get a job when she graduated in 1923.

Norine Cyrus graduated from the University of Pittsburgh in 1929. She worked at *The Pittsburgh Courier* for a while because there were no teaching positions for Blacks. She finally went into social work. In 1947, she was finally able to get a teaching position as a substitute at Robert L. Vann School.

Maxine Whedbee left Pittsburgh to teach in West
Virginia. She graduated from the University of
Pittsburgh in 1928.

Hazel Stallings graduated in 1930 and was forced to
seek a teaching position in North Carolina.

When Waunetta Alston graduated from Hampton
Institute in Virginia in 1936, she didn't even bother to
apply for a job in Pittsburgh because she knew Blacks
were not being hired by the Board of Education.

Frances Brown went to Virginia after she graduated in
1938 because she could not secure a teaching position
in Pittsburgh.

Gertrude Wade says that, when she graduated in 1944,
her counselor asked her if she was "going South to
help her people."

We will never know the full impact of these racist practices or the
names of all those who were discriminated against. We will also never
know how many Blacks were simply too discouraged to even attempt
to get the necessary education to become a teacher. What we can state
without fear of contradiction is that those Blacks who graduated as
teachers before 1937 were discriminated against by the Pittsburgh
Board of Public Education. They were forced by these practices to give
up teaching or to leave Pittsburgh.

Behind-the-scenes pressure as well as the constant pressure of *The
Pittsburgh Courier* was beginning to discomfort some members of the
Pittsburgh School Board. In 1935, after years of pressure from people
like Homer S. Brown, Richard Jones, Robert L. Vann and others, the
School Board of Pittsburgh took its first step toward the hiring of Black
teachers since the 19th century. *The Pittsburgh Courier* of February 2,
1935, carried the banner headline, "35 Apply for Jobs as City Teachers."
Another headline on March 9, 1935 announced that nine Blacks had
qualified to take the teacher's exam. Despite these tentative moves,

no Blacks were hired, and it seemed unlikely they would be hired in the near future. Because of the failure to act decisively, the Pittsburgh Board of Public Education became the target of a Legislative Hearing on alleged discriminatory hiring practices.

The Hearings

While there are no official documents to indicate the rationale for Blacks attempting to challenge the Pittsburgh School Board's hiring practices at this time, some ideas emerge from conversations with Judge Brown and Attorney Jones. According to Judge Brown and Attorney Jones, Blacks had attempted unsuccessfully to elect Black legislators during the late 1920s and early 1930s. Political news published in *The Pittsburgh Courier* indicates that local and state political leaders did not pay much attention to Black voters, because Blacks lacked political power.

A series of events took place starting in 1935 that brought the issue to a head. First, Blacks in the area finally got enough political clout to elect Homer S. Brown to the state legislature. Secondly, Brown, Jones and other Blacks had begun to discuss again what should be done about the hiring practices of the Pittsburgh School Board. It is difficult to determine who provided the impetus for the first moves, since most people tend to recall the events of the time from slightly different vantage points. However, what seems to be clear is that there was some movement toward accepting a separate Black school system which would employ Black teachers. Attorney Jones indicated that he felt this was a mistake; it would mean accepting mental slavery.

An informal group of Black leaders, apparently composed primarily of Black Democrats, said that there was no way that the Board was going to hire Blacks. Previous attempts had been unsuccessful. Attorney Jones told the group that past attempts had been piecemeal and unorganized, and that no one had made any significant effort to break the School Board's hiring practices. He said that Blacks should try a direct frontal attack on the Board.

It was out of such long discussions in 1935 and 1936 that the idea of utilizing their newfound political clout grew. As Attorney Jones put it, "We were feeling our oats."[12] Thus came the idea that Legislator Brown should introduce a resolution in the Pennsylvania House of Representatives calling for a formal legislative hearing into alleged discriminatory hiring practices of the Pittsburgh Public School Board.

Recalling the days before the hearing, Judge Brown told the author that most people were not concerned, or at least did not exhibit any concern, over the lack of Black school teachers. "Every once in a while someone would try to do something, but most people were asleep." Judge Brown felt that it was extremely important to approach the problem in the right way. A bill, even the best one, could have been rewritten and thus been rendered ineffective. If a Bill were introduced, the burden of proof would have been left up to those who challenged the Board. For this reason, Brown felt a resolution was the best approach. If the resolution was accepted, then the Board would be subpoenaed and would have to prove that it had not discriminated against Blacks. "Article 10 of the State Constitution says that the State shall authorize the operation of a public school system. My approach was constitutional. I linked Article 10 with the discrimination against Black teachers."

The question then became not so much one of morality or civil rights as it was a violation of the State Constitution. Judge Brown felt that this use of constitutional law gave Blacks the right lever to use against the School Board. This constitutional approach to civil rights was to become the hallmark of Judge Brown as he attacked discrimination in other areas.

As a result of deliberations with Dr. Charles H. Carroll of the Pittsburgh Urban League, William T. Poole of the Pittsburgh National Association for the Advancement of Colored People, and Richard F. Jones, his law partner, Judge Brown, who had been in the Pennsylvania legislature since 1935, introduced a resolution in February 1937 to investigate alleged discriminatory hiring practices of the Board of Public Education in Pittsburgh. The resolution was passed, and the entire Board of Education was subpoenaed to appear before the legislative committee. The members of the legislative committee were George J. Sarrat, Al Tronzo, L.K. Harkins, Elmer Holland, and Chairman Homer

---

12 Richard Jones in discussion with the author, 1973.

S. Brown. The attorneys whose task it was to prove the discrimination charges were Richard F. Jones and Joseph Givens.

According to Judge Brown and Richard Jones, the resolution was passed with no difficulties.[13] Why was it passed? There were probably two main reasons: first, because of the political climate of the time, which Attorney Jones describes as "New Dealist"; and second, because Blacks had exhibited enough political unity to elect a state legislator and therefore White political leaders thought that Blacks were a political force to be respected.

Attorney Jones recalled that some people were afraid that he would be unable to prove his case of discrimination against the Board. He was certain that he could prove his case in a minimal length of time. He was sure, in fact, that the Board of Education would provide its own statistics which would prove his case in a matter of seconds.[14]

Several newspapers carried stories about the upcoming hearings. *The Pittsburgh Crusader*, a second Black paper of the period, reported on February 13, 1937:

> Legislator Homer S. Brown introduced a resolution
> into the House of Representatives last Monday night
> urging an immediate investigation of the Board of
> Education here. The resolution, which is designed to
> explore the tightly held cards of the present Board
> of Education which has persistently refused to grant
> appointments to qualified race (Black) instructors,
> is expected to receive keen attention in the present
> session of the legislature.

In the February 19, 1937, edition, *The Pittsburgh Crusader* stated that the legislative committee had the power to issue subpoenas commanding person or persons to appear before it and require them to answer any proper questions and produce such books, papers or documents as the committee might deem necessary. This power would be used against the Board, *The Pittsburgh Crusader* stated and quoted an excerpt from the resolution:

---

13 Richard Jones and Homer S. Brown in discussion with the author, 1973.
14 Richard Jones in discussion with the author, 1975.

>Whereas there is not now, neither has there been in the
>past a single Negro teacher employed by said Board of
>Public Education, although many persons of said race
>have applied for said positions

>...Whereas it is alleged that the said Board of Public
>Education has steadfastly refused to employ any Negro
>teachers, said refusal being contrary to the laws of this
>Commonwealth...

In April of 1937, the hearings got underway in the City Council
Chambers in downtown Pittsburgh. The members of the Board of
Education steadfastly denied that any Black had ever been discriminated
against in their hiring practices. Dr. Ben G. Graham, Superintendent
of the Board, said there was no discrimination and further stated that
Lawrence Peeler would soon be moved up from a part-time position
to a full-time position. He did not specify what "soon" meant.[15] Upon
investigation, the author found that Lawrence Peeler had been hired
part-time in 1933 to teach choral music at night and instrumental music
during the day. From available information, it appears that he was the
only Black teacher employed in 1933 on either a full-time or part-time
basis.[16]

After learning about Mr. Peeler, Attorney Jones asked how long it
would normally take Mr. Peeler to move to a full-time position given
his present place on the eligibility roles. Dr. Graham replied, "in about
two and a half years." Dr. Graham indicated that Peeler was the first
Black he had recommended to the School Board since he became
Superintendent in 1930. He offered as evidence of non-discrimination
the fact that three Blacks had passed recent teacher exams—Saletta
Bozier, Henrietta Brogwell and James Moore Miller.[17]

Under further cross-examination by Attorney Jones, Dr. Graham
was asked how many teachers the Board employed and how many of
these full-time teachers were Black. Dr. Graham reportedly replied that

---

15 *The Pittsburgh Crusader*, May 1, 1937, page 1.
16 Lawrence Peeler in discussion with the author, 1978.
17 *The Pittsburgh Courier*, May 1, 1937, page 1.

there were 3,400 teachers, all of whom were White. Jones felt that all he had to do at this point was to prove that the lack of Black teachers was a direct result of overt discrimination.[18]

The next witness called for the School Board was Marcus Aaron, President of the Board. "I thought he was going to have a seizure when I called him as a witness," Jones said. Under examination, Aaron said that the Board had never turned down anyone recommended by the Superintendent. However, it was revealed that no Blacks had been recommended since Aaron had joined the Board in 1911. When asked whether he had any knowledge about some Black women who had qualified for teaching positions between 1915 and 1922 being told by the late school superintendent that they should "go South," Aaron replied that he had never heard of the incidents.

Aaron accused the committee of "creating a public issue where none exists." He admitted that he had never brought up the issue of hiring Blacks before the Board, because he was sure it would have "created more enemies than friends for the colored people." When asked by Al Tronzo if Blacks should be more concerned about friends than securing teaching positions, Aaron replied, "Yes, I think there are a lot more important questions for them to discuss."[19]

Mr. N.R. Criss, Board Solicitor, testified that the failure of Blacks to get appointments was not based on race but rather was one of qualification:

> Under the law, appointments are made from the three highest ranking applicants on the eligibility list. The competition for the eligibility list is severe, many of the applicants hold master's and even doctor's degrees. Up to now, no colored applicant has ever reached the top of the list. The same is true of scores of White applicants.

Mr. Maurice Moss, an Urban League official, replied that there were 700 Black teachers in New York City and hundreds in Chicago,

---

18 Richard Jones in discussion with the author, 1977.
19 *The Pittsburgh Courier*, May 8, 1937, page 1.

Cleveland, and other cities where educational requirements were as severe.[20]

Frank Bolden, Owner, *The Pittsburgh Courier* – c 1950-1970

Richard F. Jones, Attorney – 1949

---

20 *The Pittsburgh Post-Gazette*, April 23, 1937, page 1.

**Judge Homer S. Brown (far right) with wife
Wilhelmina and son Byrd – c 1940-1955**

Alma Speed Fox – c 1940-1955

During the hearings it was revealed that Solicitor Criss had written a letter to Thomas Harrison stating that the Board would never hire Negro teachers to teach White students and that to do so would be suicidal. [21] Statistics revealed during the hearings showed the following: as of 1937, there were 11,000 Black pupils in the school system; there were 3,400 full-time teachers, all of whom were White.[22] *The Bulletin Index* of April 22, 1937, said,

> Nine percent of the city's 58,000 school children are colored and although at such schools as Watt, McKelvey and Franklin Elementary a full 99% of the children are Negro, all teachers are White. Sixty-four percent of the students at Herron Hill Jr. High are colored, as are 161 of the students at Schenley High School. Elsewhere in the large eastern centers of Negro population—New York, Philadelphia, Harrisburg—colored elementary teachers, principals even, have been employed for years.

At one point in the proceedings, School Solicitor Criss said that the Board had informally considered turning over an entire school to Black students who would have been taught by an all-Black faculty. The Board was considering this move in 1914, Mr. Criss stated, but the idea was never formally considered because of opposition from the Pittsburgh Urban League.[23] When asked why he had suggested an all-Black school when this could not be done under the law, Criss replied, "We were trying to devise a way out of difficulty. I felt that Pittsburgh should have the same arrangements as Philadelphia, which has colored schools because colored people are satisfied with the condition." *The Pittsburgh Crusader* reported on April 30, 1937, that the school which the Board had considered converting was the Watt Street School in the Hill District.

It was also revealed that the Board of Education had operated a training school for teachers since 1912, but that no Blacks had been

---

21 *The Pittsburgh Post-Gazette*, April 23, 1937, page 1.
22 *The Pittsburgh Courier*, May 1, 1937, page 1.
23 *The Pittsburgh Press*, April 25, 1937, page 1.

admitted to the training school since 1922.[24] Those Blacks who had graduated from their Teacher Training School had been unable to secure appointments in Pittsburgh, as was shown during the hearings. Georgine Pearce Brown graduated from the training school in 1920. She had been trained as a kindergarten teacher. During the hearings Mrs. Pearce said she had graduated first in a class of eight; all others were hired (they were White), while she was not. She also said that Mrs. Edna Jefferson, another Black woman who finished in the same year as an elementary teacher, was the only person in her graduating class who was not hired by the Pittsburgh Board of Education.[25]

When asked by the author how she knew she was first in her class, Mrs. Pearce stated that she had received a letter from the Board indicating her position in the class. She said that she had produced the letter at the 1937 hearings to back up her statement. She talked further about her experiences. "In the last part of our training we were to receive five months of practice teaching. I received the full five months, but other Blacks before me either got no practice teaching or got very little." According to Mrs. Pearce, most Black graduates of the training school were sent to the Irene Kaufmann Center in the Hill, where the Board was operating a school for children suffering from tuberculosis. When her supervisor talked with Mrs. Pearce just before graduation, the conference was held in private, although the usual procedure was to assign practice teachers in pairs and to hold the final conference with both students present. During the conference, Mrs. Pearce was informed that she would not get a job in Pittsburgh because the Board did not hire colored teachers.[26]

Mrs. Pearce secured a position with the Pittsburgh Urban League as a Home and School Visitor in the Hill and East Liberty. During that time, she had the opportunity to talk to or see all the other women who had graduated with her class. All of them, with the exception of Edna Jefferson, who also was Black, were employed as teachers in the Pittsburgh Public School system. According to Mrs. Pearce, Edna Jefferson had gone to Philadelphia to join the segregated teaching staff there.

---

24 *The Pittsburgh Sun Telegraph*, April 25, 1937, page 1.
25 *The Pittsburgh Courier*, May 1, 1937, page 1.
26 Georgine Pearce Brown in discussion with the author, 1973.

The hearings also showed that Vivian Pollard Robinson and Helen Miller had graduated from the Board-operated training school in 1919 as elementary teachers. Neither got a job. Mary Woods, another Black woman, graduated in 1922 and she, like the others, was not offered employment by the Board. Helen Morrison talked to the author about her experiences with the training school. Her White classmates would call her after graduation to indicate that they had gotten teaching positions in the Pittsburgh Public Schools. They would say, "But you graduated way ahead of me. Why didn't you get your appointment?" Mrs. Miller and her father went to see Superintendent Davidson of the Pittsburgh Board of Education to talk to him about the reasons for Mrs. Miller's being denied a job. Davidson attempted to placate them by saying that he would try to secure a position for her in Indianapolis, Indiana. He felt certain, he said, that his friend, who was the superintendent of the Indianapolis school system, would give her a job because they already employed a large number of "colored teachers."[27]

Another witness against the School Board, Dr. Ulysses Williams, testified that his daughter had been denied admission to the training school even though she had graduated at the head of her class from Schenley High School in 1936. She took the exam for the training school and finished in fourth place. She was turned down by the school's medical board, even though exams ordered by her physician father before and after her entrance exam proved her to be in excellent health.

Yet another witness testified about the Board's discrimination. Mrs. Alice Smith testified that her sister, Eleanor Haynes, was a graduate of the first class of the Pittsburgh training school. She, too, was passed over when appointments were made.[28]

By the end of the second hearing session, Richard Jones, Homer Brown, and others were convinced that the Board had indeed discriminated against Blacks. Among the committee's findings were:

1. That from 1915 to 1922, there was sufficient evidence to indicate direct discrimination against Negro teachers.

2. That since the new eligibility requirements of 1932, although

---

27 Helen Miller in discussion with the author, 1973.
28 *The Pittsburgh Courier*, May 1, 1937, page 1.

the evidence of discrimination is not as clear and direct as in the previous period, nevertheless from the sum total of all the evidence sufficient proof has been presented to conclude that the allegation (discrimination) has been substantiated.

3. That since 1922 no Blacks had been admitted to the Training School from which the Board takes 60% of its new teachers.

4. That the lack of action on the part of the School Board was not due to lack of knowledge but to the desire of the Board not to consider the issue.[29]

At the conclusion of the hearing, Dr. Davidson stated that Lawrence Peeler would be hired as a full-time teacher by the Board by September of 1937.[30] It will be recalled that early in the investigation Dr. Davidson had said that it would ordinarily take Mr. Peeler "about two and a half years" to move up to the top of the eligibility list. Was the move to hire Peeler a direct result of the hearings? Had the Board given in to public pressure? Both Judge Brown and Richard Jones think that, as a result of the wide media coverage and the resultant pressure of the negative public information, the Pittsburgh Public School Board had to address itself to the issue of hiring Blacks.

The Pittsburgh Courier of June 5, 1937, hailed the victory in banner headlines, "School Board Guilty of Flagrant Discrimination." So the Board of Education had been found guilty as charged. What remained was to await the response of the Board of Education.

Summary and Conclusions

In 1837, after pressure from the Black community in Pittsburgh, the Board of Education relented and formed two all-Black "colored schools." Later, the schools, which had been bounced around the city from church basements to fire engine stations, were located in a new facility on Miller Street. From then on, it was referred to as "The Colored School." Blacks were employed in the school as teachers, and until 1867 they received a smaller salary than teachers in other city

---

29 *The Pittsburgh Press*, June 3, 1937, page 1.
30 *The Pittsburgh Courier*, June 5, 1937.

schools. In 1881, the "colored school" was closed forever, and Black students entered a more or less integrated school system. The same cannot be said for Black teachers, because from that time until 1937, there would be no Black teachers hired by the Pittsburgh Board of Public Education.

For many of the intervening years, Blacks agitated for the Board of Education to hire Black teachers, but to no avail. Finally, in 1937, the Board members were subpoenaed by the Pennsylvania House of Representatives to appear before a committee investigating racial discrimination in the hiring of teachers in the Pittsburgh Public School system.

It is apparent that the Pittsburgh Board of Education discriminated against Black students and teachers in the 19th century, first by ignoring the need for educating Black youngsters and secondly by setting up an inferior and separate school system for Black students. Finally, they hired only a few Black teachers and assigned them only to the "colored schools." The discrimination continued after the "colored school" was closed—from that time until 1937, the Board refused to hire Black teachers, even though qualified Blacks were available. As a result of this refusal, the Board was forced to try to prove that it hired on a non- discriminatory basis before a Pennsylvania State committee investigating racial discrimination in the hiring of Black teachers.

In 1937, the Pennsylvania State House of Representatives held a legislative hearing in Pittsburgh. The purpose of this hearing was to investigate alleged discriminatory hiring practices of the Pittsburgh Board of Public Education. Witnesses were called both from the Board and from Pittsburgh's Black community.

The Board denied that it had discriminated against Blacks by claiming that it had been unable to find qualified Black candidates for teaching positions. The Black witnesses called, however, wove a tight web of evidence proving that the Board had indeed discriminated against Blacks in its hiring practices. The committee agreed with the witnesses against the Board, and concluded that the Board had practiced racially discriminatory hiring since 1911.

The evidence presented during the hearing showed several patterns of discrimination. The first involved the refusal to hire Black teachers even after they had been graduated from the teacher training school operated by the Board. This practice continued for a number of years.

The second pattern of discrimination involved closing the doors of the teacher training school to all Blacks, thus making it more difficult for Blacks to gain access.to the school system, since 60% of the teachers hired in Pittsburgh came from this in-house teacher training school.

The final pattern appears to have been not hiring teachers unless they were recommended by the Superintendent of Pittsburgh Public Schools. The discrimination came into focus when it was revealed that the Superintendent had never seen fit to recommend a Black teacher. Throughout the hearings, the Board had maintained that it could find "no qualified Blacks."

Thus, from 1837 to 1937, the Public School system had gone full circle. Prior to 1837, there were no Black teachers. Yielding to pressure from the Black community, the Board hired some Blacks to teach in the then all-Black school system. After the "colored schools" were closed in 1881, the Board stopped hiring Black teachers on a full-time basis until again, in response to pressure from the Black community, the Board hired its first full-time Black teacher in the 20th century in 1937.

CHAPTER 3

External Pressure: The Cracks in the Wall

In the preceding chapters, the wall of discrimination erected by Pittsburgh against Blacks was shown. It is obvious that Blacks faced discrimination on nearly every front—in housing, employment, education, and public accommodations.

In Chapter 2, the pattern of discrimination against Black teachers since the beginning of the Pittsburgh Public School system was shown. That wall of discrimination consisted first of hiring Black teachers for a separate "colored" school system; then excluding Blacks from teaching positions when the "colored" system closed in 1881.

In this chapter we will examine the first "cracks" in the wall, the trickle of a few Black teachers into the mainstream, and what happened to them. This chapter will also trace the rise in that teacher population and the patterns of racism they faced.

Discrimination in Other Cities

Before examining discrimination against Black teachers in Pittsburgh, it is helpful to briefly examine discrimination against Blacks in other cities. As has been stated elsewhere in this paper, other cities had employed Black teachers before Pittsburgh. While this is true, it also true that Blacks were not treated fairly in most of those cities. C. Wilson Record, speaking of California, says:

> Recent reports (1963) issued by the State Department
> of Education showed that members of certain ethnic
> minorities, particularly Negroes, were not hired in

some districts. Out of 708 school districts reporting in a survey in 1959, only 16% had employed one or more Black school teachers during the past 10 years.

The article quoted a school superintendent in a northern California town who said,

> Any Negro teacher whom we would even seriously consider would have to be truly outstanding. The Negro applicant would have to be truly outstanding. The Negro applicant would have to be better, a lot better than the average white teacher on our staff; he would need to be in a non-sensitive subject area—say chemistry, math or metal shop—and he would have to have personality plus.

In speaking of school board hiring practices, the article states:

> Crucial here is the fact that the hiring agencies are local school boards--not the federal government, not the state, not even the county. School boards are reflections of and spokesmen for local community attitudes and values and institutions. More specifically, they are political entities through which power groups in the community express their interests and preferences. School boards also tend to be highly provincial in character, zealously guarding their boundaries and prerogatives, and yielding only reluctantly to the broader demands of the state and nation with complex public problems and policies. School boards tend to be conservative, they are not innovators except within certain narrow areas of curriculum and administration . . . perhaps the greatest reluctance of school boards, weak or strong, is to be found in the initial hiring of Negro teachers. Most of them would regard this as an extremely bold step to which there is likely to be a strong adverse reaction, this in spite of the favorable

experiences that other districts taking the plunge have had. Board members explain their reluctance in a number of ways: no well qualified Negroes have applied; the students would be disturbed by the presence of a Negro teacher; other teachers are prejudiced and would not like to serve with Negroes.[1]

In Indianapolis in 1949, where there were still some all-Black schools, there was a tendency to retain the idea that Blacks should teach Blacks and Whites should teach in mixed or all-White schools. The desegregation of teachers took place after the desegregation of students. As of 1950, Black teachers were placed only in elementary schools. The elementary schools that they were placed in had either all- Black or mixed student populations. No Black teachers had yet been assigned to the schools having all-White populations. Neither had Blacks been placed in the mixed high schools. Some had been placed in the all-Black high schools.

In Indiana as a whole, the only place where complete integration of faculties had taken place was in certain small, rural communities which had completely eliminated segregated schools and in which all Black teachers had tenure before desegregation.[2]

When New York discontinued statutory segregation in 1873, no Black teachers were hired for nearly 22 years.[3] As was shown earlier, the same thing happened in Pittsburgh: when segregated education was discontinued in 1881, no Black teachers were hired for 56 years.

David Tyack says, "One measure of the willingness of school systems to counteract racism in the job market was the hiring of Black teachers and other employees. Most systems failed this test badly."[4] Tyack goes on to state that there was no shortage of trained Black teachers, especially in view of the fact that there were many training programs for Black teachers in both the North and South. Tyack also

1 C. Wilson Record, "School Board and Negro Teachers in California," *Integrated Education* 1, no. 2 (April 1963): excerpts from 20, 21, 22 respectively.
2 Dwight W. Culver, "Racial Desegregation in Education in Indiana," *Journal of Negro Education*, 3 (1954): 301.
3 David B. Tyack, *The One Best System, A History of American Urban Education* (Cambridge: Harvard University Press, 1974), 117.
4 Tayack, 225.

echoes my findings about Pittsburgh, when he states that precise data about Black teachers in Northern cities is impossible to find since most schools did not list teachers by race.

In 1970, the United States Senate held hearings on Equal Educational Opportunity in the United States. Part of the resulting report said:

> It is clear that in the past Negro teachers were employed specifically and exclusively for the purpose of teaching Negro pupils in racially segregated schools. Segregated schools required segregated student bodies taught by segregated faculties ....If considerable numbers of Negroes resided in a school district, the usual procedure was to provide for all practical purposes a separate school system for the... Since Negro teachers were employed to teach Negro pupils, there were relatively few positions for Negro teachers in a system with few Negro classrooms. In a system with no classes for Negroes there were no positions for Negro teachers.[5]

As we can see from these examples, Boards of Education around the country used a variety of methods to thwart the attempts of Blacks to gain equal employment as school teachers, but that they had begun to hire Black teachers before the Pittsburgh school board. The question arises: Why was Pittsburgh slower in hiring Black teachers than many other cities? The author posed this question to several of Pittsburgh's early Black teachers. Most replied simply that Pittsburgh was usually behind any other major city when it came to making progress, especially when that progress had anything to do with Blacks.

The evidence suggests that the question cannot be that simply dismissed. From the information gathered for this study, several reasons suggest themselves. One is the relative ease with which the Central Board of Education was able to close the "colored" school in 1881. The lack of any organized protest on the part of Blacks in Pittsburgh

5 "Hearings before the Select Committee on Equal Educational Opportunity of the United States Senate. Ninety-first Congress, Second Session, On Equal Educational Opportunity," (U.S. Government Printing Office, 1970), 1104.

at that time (although Blacks had resisted previous attempts to close the school) allowed those individuals who controlled Pittsburgh public education to assume that Blacks did not care about who taught their children. It was a fact that there were no Black teachers in any of the other schools in Pittsburgh. In view of this, perhaps the members of the Board assumed that Blacks cared more about the education of their children than they did about the employment of Black teachers.

A second reason for Pittsburgh's slowness rests in the fact that most of the potential Black teachers did not protest. This lack of pressure from qualified teachers eased the burden on the Board. Black teachers were not protesting in any significant degree because those who wanted to teach found employment in other cities, albeit on a segregated basis. Other qualified teachers settled down in other occupations.

The lack of unity in the Black community also made organized protest difficult, especially around the latter part of the 19th and early part of the 20th century. Unlike many cities, Pittsburgh did not and does not have one large Black community; rather, it has many. Those Black communities changed over time, at one time being located on Ross Street, in what is now the downtown area, and at another time at 32nd and Smallman Streets in what became the Strip district. There are also long-standing Black communities in Oakland, the Hill, East Liberty, Homewood, Beltzhoover, the North Side, and the West End. These scattered communities made protest on an organized basis extremely difficult.

While it is difficult to reconstruct early National Association for the Advancement of Colored People activities in Pittsburgh prior to 1937, it is evident that the organization was not deeply involved in the issue of hiring Black teachers. Neither was any other organization, for that matter. Many Blacks were concerned with maintaining a picture of propriety. Public protest was considered unacceptable.

Another factor contributing to the Pittsburgh Board's delay is the split in the Black community that was discussed previously. Had there been agreement as to whether Blacks should push for the hiring of teachers in an integrated or segregated school system, the early hiring of Black teachers might have been facilitated.

Finally, had Blacks opted for the separate school system in the early 1900s, it is almost certain that Black teachers would have been hired prior to 1937. It will be recalled that the Pittsburgh Board had considered turning over Watt Street School to Blacks in the early 1900s. Had Blacks accepted this offer, it is likely that Pittsburgh would have begun to hire Black teachers at about the same time that other major cities did.

Therefore, it seems, from an examination of existing evidence, that there were many contributing factors to the apparent "snail's pace" hiring of Black teachers by the Pittsburgh Board of Public Education.

Success at Last –
Board Hires First Black Teacher in the Twentieth Century

As a result of the 1937 Pennsylvania Legislative Hearing into the discriminatory hiring practices of the Board of Education, the first full-time Black teacher was hired since the mid-19th century. In the September 21, 1937, minutes of the Board of Education, the notation appears under the teacher appointment section: "Peeler, Paul Lawrence, July 21, 1933 - Teacher Watt School at the salary of $1,300.00 to date from September 1, 1937."[6] Mr. Peeler was hired as an itinerant music teacher traveling to schools in the Hill.

In a *Pittsburgh Press* article, Mr. Peeler was quoted about his impressions of the early 1900s as far as

Black teachers were concerned. In those days, you had to be hired from an eligibility list.

> In order to get on that list, not only did you have to score well on the tests, but you also had to have experience, they said. So Black teachers had to leave the city to get experience, usually at Black schools in the South. But the white teachers who didn't have experience could get hired. Blacks had to play by a different set of rules then. But to be fair about it, the Board wasn't too interested in hiring Catholics or Jews for teaching jobs in those days either. Those jobs were for WASPs.[7]

---

6 Minutes, Pittsburgh Board of Education, September 21, 1937.
7 *The Pittsburgh Press*, Roto Section, June 6, 1976.

Mr. Peeler told the author that prejudice against ethnic groups and Catholics and Jews was nearly as strong as that against Blacks. Consequently, only White Protestants had an easy time finding teaching jobs. In conversations with the author, Mr. Peeler said that it was not easy getting on that eligibility list. He had to take the exam three times in order to get up on that list."[8]

Mr. Peeler said he had spent four years as a part-time teacher of music preparing himself for becoming a full-time teacher. When asked how he had been allowed to teach even on a part-time basis, he indicated that he had begun his practice teaching in 1932. The Board didn't fear him because he was a musician, and music was a field that Blacks were accepted in—at least to some extent. Peeler felt that had he been a math teacher instead of a musician he might never have gotten the opportunity to be the first Black teacher, in this century, to be hired on a full-time, basis.

Peeler had asked that, as an extra part of his practice teaching, he be allowed to try teaching choral music. Apparently this was an acceptable area, since many Whites readily accepted the "quaint" religious music Blacks sang. The Board agreed to let Peeler teach choral music under the direction of a Black man, Rogers Walker, who was a custodian at the Pittsburgh Musical Institute on Bellefield Avenue. According to Peeler, Mr. Walker had probably asked to be allowed to study musical composition. "They probably told him 'no' but you can be where it is taught and perhaps you can pick up on it as you sweep the floors.[9] Walker accepted the position of custodian, learned what he could about musical composition, and formed a Black choral group.

Peeler eventually took over the group, which was held in the "Americanization schools"—schools where recent immigrants were taught American English. Peeler recalls that these schools were: Larimer in East Liberty, which served the Italian immigrants; Watt Street School in the Hill, which served the Jewish population; and Conroy School on the North Side, which served the Russian and Polish immigrants.

In recalling those choral sessions, Peeler said that the only music the immigrants heard in those buildings was Blacks singing. "I would

---

8 The comments in the following paragraphs are drawn from the author's discussion with Lawrence Peeler in 1978.
9 Lawrence Peeler in discussion with author, 1978.

have my group sing some of their (the immigrants') folk songs and they (the authorities) would let the immigrants come and stand outside the room to listen but they wouldn't let them come inside. They were teaching those people prejudice—stay away from those Black people."

In addition to teaching the choral classes, Peeler taught instrumental music on a part-time basis during the day. He taught at Minersville, Rose Street and Watt Street Schools in the Hill, Conroy on the North Side, and Larimer in East Liberty. The children paid 25 cents each for the lessons. He had asked to be allowed to teach at Herron Hill Jr. High School, but was refused by a Board of Education member who said, "I wouldn't think about recommending you for Herron Hill, because you might try to have as good an orchestra as my children have at Taylor Alderdice."

Peeler became involved in this part-time teaching effort because he wanted to take the exam to become a permanent teacher. A candidate needed three years of experience to take the permanent teacher exam. "Often that was a moot point," Peeler said, "since many Blacks had gone away and taught for three years and came back and still weren't allowed to take the test."

Despite his efforts, it seems apparent that, had it not been for the 1937 hearings, it is likely that Peeler would have had to wait until 1939 or 1940 to become a full-time teacher if, in fact, the Board had moved by that time to hire Blacks on a full-time basis.

When asked how he was treated by his fellow teachers, Mr. Peeler indicated that, on the whole, he was treated pretty well by White teachers. Perhaps one of the reasons was that Mr. Peeler was in the position of teaching a subject that was not overly threatening to most teachers – music.

Black musicians were, by and large, acceptable to White society. Perhaps Mr. Peeler's acceptance would have been different had he been employed to teach an academic subject, such as science or math or a foreign language.

While Mr. Peeler felt that he himself was accorded respect, he did not feel that the same held true for Black students. According to Mr. Peeler, most White teachers seemed to feel that Black students were backward. He recalled one incident in which he had visited a music class in Lincoln School in East Liberty. The teacher told him that some of the kids, especially two Black brothers, were exceptionally slow. When Peeler asked the Black youngsters to play something for him, the teacher interjected that they were so slow that they could not read music and would only embarrass him if they tried. Peeler insisted, and the two brothers played a highly complex jazz composition written by Duke Ellington. Peeler found that the youngsters never bothered to learn to read music because they had the gift of being able to play by ear. One of these "backward" Black youngsters was Erroll Garner, the world-famous jazz pianist.

Blacks in the city hoped that the hiring of Peeler in 1937 marked the end of discrimination against Black teachers. They also hoped that their hiring would signal the beginning of a rapid growth in the Black teacher population in the city. Both hopes proved unfounded. The Board of Education in Pittsburgh would simply substitute another form of discrimination for the practice of not hiring Blacks at all, which would continue well into the 1970s, even though the Black student population continued to rise throughout the whole time period.

The Crack Widens – More Black Teachers Hired

In 1938, Antoinette Westmoreland Brown was hired by the Board of Education. Ms. Brown, technically speaking, was not a teacher. She was listed by the Board as an activities director, and was employed at the Herron Hill Jr. High School.

In 1939, the Board hired its third Black professional—another music teacher—James Miller. Dr. Earhart, the Director of Music for the Board, approached Mr. Peeler to supervise Miller's practice teaching. Earhart said that, if Peeler did not do the supervision, it would be difficult to find a White teacher who would be willing to take the job. Peeler himself had been supervised by people who knew him and knew his family. Unfortunately, the author was not able to obtain information from Brown or Miller, since they died prior to the writing of this study.

While it is certain who the first three Black professionals hired by the Pittsburgh Board of Education were, it becomes nearly impossible from this point on to do a completely accurate reconstruction of the sequence of Black hirings because of the absence of accurate record-keeping on the part of the Pittsburgh Board of Education. If such records were kept by race, they never saw the light of day and are at this time not part of the public record. The author was told by one retired Board official that, in the early days, when they wanted to know how many Black teachers there were someone simply got on the telephone and called all the principals and asked for a head count. The gentleman, who wished not to be named, said that everyone knew how many Blacks there were because of the ease with which the small number could be counted. While the published minutes of the Board of Education do provide a list of the names and dates of teacher appointments, no mention is made of the race of the appointees. Furthermore, when records were kept by race, all Black professionals were usually lumped under one heading, making it nearly impossible to determine how many of the professionals were teachers. Therefore, while it is certain who some of these early teachers were, it is not certain whether all of them were counted. It is not necessary to totally reconstruct the hiring practices of the School Board to reveal the fact that Black teachers were the victims of racial discrimination practiced by the Board of Education.

In 1943, the Pittsburgh School Board reported that it had in its employ four full-time Black employees: two elementary school teachers, one non-teaching Black employee in the secondary school system, and one Black employee in the Compulsory Attendance Department.[10] It is certain that the two elementary teachers were Mr. Peeler and Mr. Miller. The Black employed at the secondary level was Mrs. Jones.

It is not known who the other full-time Black employee was. It is evident that, from 1937 to 1942, the Board had only hired two Black teachers--both musicians and both elementary school teachers.

Referring to the above statistics, the 1943 State Commission on Urban Colored Population, which had been commissioned by the state government to study the situation of Blacks in urban Pennsylvania, said:

> Obviously these positions are hardly enough to be
> called "token" appointments and can be regarded only
> as a very small beginning. As the system expands

---

10 Report of the Pennsylvania State Temporary Commission on Urban Colored Populations, 1943, page 410.

and as white teachers resign or retire, competent Negro teachers should be appointed immediately until the number of Negro teachers becomes somewhat proportionate to the Negro's ratio in the general population.[11]

It would be many years before Blacks in Pittsburgh would even approach this goal.

In an untitled working paper from the Temporary Commission on Urban Colored, found in the personal papers of Wilhelmina Byrd Brown (Mrs. Homer S. Brown), the author found the following statement:

> ...a casual review will show that in the field of education, four Negro teachers for the first time have been employed by the Pittsburgh Board of Education. No one claims that suddenly these four teachers became endowed with sufficient mentality to be the only Negroes to qualify as teachers.
>
> The undisputed fact is that for years the School Board actually carried out its policy that only white teachers were eligible to teach in our schools, not withstanding the laws of the Commonwealth to the contrary.[12]

How did Pittsburgh compare with other cities in 1940? According to David B. Tyack, Doxey Wilkerson gathered the information about Black teachers presented in Table 3-1. As we can see, Pittsburgh was far behind any comparably-sized city cited in the survey.

After the 1937 legislative hearing, there was apparently little activity on the part of the local civil rights group concerning Black teachers. From *Pittsburgh Courier* accounts and from conversations with those involved in the 1937 hearings, as well as others, it seems that most people simply assumed that, since it had been proved that

---

11 Report of the Pennsylvania State Temporary Commission on Urban Colored Populations, 1943, page 411.
12 Untitled working paper of the Pennsylvania State Temporary Commission on Urban Colored Populations, undated, page 3.

the Pittsburgh Board of Education practiced discrimination, a regular hiring process for Black teachers would be established. This was not the case. From all available information, it appears that after hiring one teacher in 1937 and one in 1939, the Board of Education did not hire any more Black teachers until 1941. As will be explained, the teachers who were hired in 1941 were not hired as regular teachers.

TABLE 3-1* NUMBER OF BLACK PROFESSIONAL EMPLOYEES (INCLUDING TEACHERS) BY CITY & POPULATION		
CITY	**BLACK**	
	POPULATION	**PROFESSIONAL STAFF**
New York	327,706	800+
Chicago	233,903	300+
Detroit	120,066	80**
Cleveland	71,899	78
Cincinnati	47,818	148
Los Angeles	38,894	54**
Newark	38,880	11
Columbus	32,774	75
Springfield	20,000	0
Dayton	17,077	80
Pittsburgh	54,938	3
* Tyack, 225. **Approximate number		

George Wilson *(seated front row, center)*; **Elmo Calloway** *(behind Wilson)*; **George Forshay** *(back row, center)* – **1963**

University of Pittsburgh Graduates *(from left)*: **Ernest A. Huddle, Russell C. Phillips, and William J. Gaskins** – **June 1951**

In the 1940s and 1950s, juvenile delinquency was a major problem in the Hill District. Most of the trouble centered around a network of organized groups. These gangs—calling themselves by such names as the Amboy Dukes, the Monarchs, the Cherokees, the Comanches and the Cobras—caused many after-school fights, created discipline problems. They ruled over the city playground areas and their drinking and gambling made the playground areas a dangerous place for younger Black children.

Apparently, sometime in 1941 the city leaders and members of the Board of Education decided to try an experiment in gang control. Since gang problems and juvenile delinquency seemed to increase dramatically during the summer months, it was decided that one way to counteract the problem was to provide youngsters with something to do during the summer months. The approach taken was to keep the public school playgrounds and gyms open during the summer for organized recreational activities.

While the idea of keeping the gyms and playgrounds open seemed good, it was not without problems. The major problem was that most Whites were afraid to deal with Black youngsters outside of the relatively safe normal school environment. It was decided that perhaps young Black teachers, who were trained in physical education, might better be able to handle the children. Therefore, the Board sought out and hired six Black teachers to work the playgrounds during the summer months. The teachers hired were:

John Brewer	McKelvy School, Hill District
John Morton	Miller School, Hill District
George Poe	Rose Street School, Hill District
Ruth Williams	Madison School, Hill District
Marian Stanton	Minersville School, Hill District
Pamela Fountain	Robert L. Vann School, Hill District[13]

John Brewer feels that, if it had not been for the juvenile delinquency problem, he and the other teachers may have had to wait much longer for a chance to be hired. "They needed Blacks who were able to

---

13 The information on the summer programs and gang problems was provided by John Brewer in discussion with the author, 1976.

handle rough ghetto kids. That's why we were hired." He also stated that no Whites wanted the job and they probably would not have been successful at any rate. The Black youngsters who were the problem simply were not going to respond to Whites. In fact, Brewer said he felt that Whites would have been in physical danger had they attempted to work the summer program.

All of the six Black teachers who were hired were successful in working with the Black youngsters. They gained the respect of the kids, counseled them, befriended them and turned many to more positive expressions of their high energy levels—such as organized athletics. While they were successful in working with the youngsters and providing a safe environment for Black youngsters in gyms and on playgrounds, the task was not always easy.

Brewer relates one incident which occurred on his first day at McKelvy School. Some Black teenagers who controlled the playground were ejected because they were drinking wine and shooting craps. After they were ejected, they returned with their leader who said to Mr. Brewer, "I'm going to kick, your ass." The teenager did, in fact, attempt to carry out his threat. Though Brewer was hesitant to describe the ensuing confrontation in detail, he did smile and say, "I tried to break his neck." Having been unsuccessful in beating Brewer physically, the teenager became a regular and friendly visitor to the playground, without the wine, the dice or the trouble.

The other Black teachers were also successful in dealing with the Black gangs in their areas. They, too, ran highly successful summer recreation programs. As a result of their successful efforts, Stanton, Poe, Williams and Brewer were allowed to apply for positions as day-to-day substitute teachers for the 1942 academic year. Some of these same individuals were later given evening assignments running recreation programs at schools which had all-Black evening programs.

In talking about his early experiences at McKelvy School, Brewer attributed his remarkable success with the tougher Black youngsters to the fact that he (Brewer) was himself raised in a Black area and was a "street person." Since he had established a reputation for not "taking any stuff" on his playground, Brewer had little further trouble with the kids in the area. Parents responded positively to his work with the youngsters, especially those parents who had been having problems with their own children.

While he indicated positive relationships with the children and parents, Brewer had some problems with his peers. As the first Black assigned to McKelvy School, he had anticipated some difficulties. White teachers were either cordial when they came into contact with him or they simply ignored him. However, Brewer indicated that he used to find notes stuck under his office door saying "Nigger, pick up your broom." Sometimes he found bags of human defecation placed on his desk by someone in the school.

In 1943, Brewer was assigned to Robert L. Vann School (also in the Hill) as a permanent substitute in the areas of physical education and hygiene. He was well accepted at Vann because many of the white teachers were afraid of the Black students and therefore welcomed the presence of a Black male teacher. His reputation as a "no-nonsense" person had preceded him to Vann. As a result, he was treated quite well by the white administration, faculty and staff.

This author remembers John Brewer quite well from his own days as a student at Vann School. On one occasion, the author was told by a gang member, "Don't start no fights while you're at the [summer] playground or Mr. Brewer will kick your ass." The author also recalls that Brewer provided a much-needed inspiration for Black youngsters, like myself. We finally had a Black role model with which we could proudly identify. One of the biggest goals of all the young Black males in the school was to become a member of Mr. Brewer's safety patrol.

What is interesting about the appointment of this second group of Blacks hired by the Board in 1941 is that all of them were physical education teachers (an area in which Blacks were more acceptable than so-called "academic" positions). Secondly, they were all appointed to positions in Hill District schools.

In 1944, John Brewer became a full-time permanent teacher in the public school system. He was one of the first Blacks to be appointed as a full-time professional employee of the Board of Education. Other Blacks assigned during the 1940s are listed in Table 3-2. Due to the lack of data, it cannot be said that these were the only Blacks appointed during that time. It is certain, however, that they were appointed in a discriminatory manner, as will be discussed later.

TABLE 3-2* BLACK TEACHERS EMPLOYED BY THE PITTSBURGH BOARD OF EDUCATION DURING THE 1940S		
YEAR	**NAME**	**SCHOOL**
1941	Frances Brown	Leo Weil
1944	Gertrude Wade	Leo Weil
1945	Emma Florine Robinson	Robert L. Vann
1945	Helen Peeler	Herron Hill Jr. High
1945	James Peeler	Herron Hill Jr. High
1946	Hazel Stallings	Robert L. Vann
1946	Waunetta Alston	Fifth Avenue Sr. High
1946	Jody Harris	Herron Hill Jr. High
1946	Leo Woods	Herron Hill Jr. High
1947	William Nicholson	Robert L. Vann
1947	Norine Cyrus	Robert L. Vann
1947	Ernestine Parks	Leo Weil
1947	Audia Mae Gilliard	Herron Hill Jr. High
1947	Elmo Calloway	Herron Hill Jr. High
1948	Mary Louise Stone	Fifth Avenue Sr. High
Compiled from personal interviews conducted by author from 1973-1975.		

Data obtained from the Pittsburgh Board of Education, indicating approximate numbers for Blacks employed as professional staff by the Board of Education, are shown in Table 3-3. No breakdown was available as to whether the Blacks were employed as teachers only or in other capacities. The personnel director emphasized that these numbers were approximations obtained by calling principals of various schools and asking them to do a physical "head count" of Black staff.

TABLE 3-3* BLACK PROFESSIONALS EMPLOYED BY BOARD OF EDUCATION IN THE 1940S	
YEAR	**# PROFESSIONALS**
1942	3
1943	3
1944	10
1945	25
1946	27
1947	30
1948	48
1949	50

*Compiled from information provided by the Pittsburgh Board of Education, Office of Personnel

Some of these early teachers spoke to the author about their treatment during these years. Gertrude Wade said that while she was treated pretty well by White staff people at A. Leo Weil, there were some people who were not very receptive to her presence. Frances Brown, who also taught at Weil, indicated that for the most part she was treated pretty well by the staff at Weil. Ernestine Parks, however, said that when she went to A. Leo Weil in 1947, she found that many of the White teachers, while not overtly hostile, would not mix with Black teachers. She felt that there were no common bonds and few, if any, friendships between Black and White teachers.[14]

Treatment of the Black teachers assigned to Robert L. Vann School in the 1940s varied. William Nicholson indicated no problems with teachers except for one, who was openly "cool" toward his presence. Hazel Stallings said that she had applied to do her student teaching at Herron Hill Jr. High, but was refused permission because of her race. She was forced to take her student teaching at A. Leo Weil in the Hill District. When she graduated from college in 1930, she had to leave Pittsburgh because the Board was not hiring Blacks then. She taught instead in North Carolina, returning to Pittsburgh in 1946. When she

---

14 Gertrude Wade, Frances Brown, and Ernestine Parks in discussions with the author, 1973.

was assigned to Vann School, she said that "White teachers treated me like I was from Mars or outer space."[15] They also appeared to dislike the fact that the students liked Mrs. Stallings and that she always appeared to be happy. She also stated that the principal at the school was racist and gave White teachers more free periods than he gave Blacks. He openly practiced favoritism toward White teachers. Mrs. Stallings stayed at Vann for 26 years, until her retirement in 1972. When asked why she had not accepted offers of transfer, she said, "Those were my kids and I loved them."

Mrs. Emma Florine Robinson was assigned as a permanent teacher at Robert L. Vann in 1946. She said that she was accepted pretty well by her peers, but was totally ignored by one teacher. As has already been mentioned, Mr. John Brewer was well accepted at the school. Norine Cyrus said Whites treated them as if they were a novelty, but did not seem to take them seriously as teachers or peers. Apparently Black teachers were a thing to be tolerated, but were of no importance.[16]

At least six Black teachers were assigned to Herron Hill Jr. High during the 1940s: Helen Peeler, (sister of Lawrence Peeler}, James Brewer (brother of John Brewer), Jody Harris, Leo Woods, Elmo Calloway and Audia Mae Gilliard. The author was able to interview four of these teachers. Jody Harris indicated no difficulty with any of the teachers or staff at Herron Hill. He said his ease of acceptance probably had a great deal to do with the fact that he was now working with some of the same people who had been his teachers when he was a student at the school. Parents respected him and students looked up to him as a positive image of a Black man. He was treated well by both Black and White students.

Audia Mae Gilliard was a regular substitute at Herron Hill in 1947. In 1948, she became a permanent teacher in the area of home economics. She indicated that the White faculty was kind of clannish, but didn't bother you. Thus, again, the practice of "benign neglect" is evident.[17]

Leo Woods, who taught English and social studies, said he was treated well by the staff and faculty at Herron Hill. He felt, however,

---

15　William Nicholson and Hazel Stallings in discussions with the author, 1973.
16　Emma Florine Robinson and Norine Cyrus in discussions with the author, 1973.
17　Audia Mae Gilliard in discussion with the author, 1973.

that there were instances in which the .administration took advantage of Black teachers by assigning them the most difficult students or requiring extra work of them. He too, however, could recall an incident with at least one White teacher. One day he walked into the teachers' room and sat down. Soon a White teacher came into the room and said, "That's my seat; I've been sitting there for years." Elmo Calloway recalls no bad incidents. All indicated that parents seemed to accept them and that they had no unusual problems with students that could be attributed to race.[18]

The first Black teachers at Fifth Avenue High School were Waunetta Alston and Mary Louise Stone. Mrs. Alston was the first Black teacher assigned to a high school in the city. She recalled that the White teachers were "not so nice." She said that, while some of them might come and ask your advice during school hours, they would not even say "hello" to you if they saw you outside the school building.

Mary Stone said that a few white teachers accepted the Blacks, but others "could not stand them."[19]

Treatment of Black teachers in the 1940s ranged from complete acceptance to rejection. Some were treated well while others experienced hostility. Others felt that whites simply ignored them. This difference in treatment of Black teachers can be seen in reference to both the staff and faculty as well as the administration.

Of the Black teachers hired by the Board of Education by the end of the 1940s, many were assigned to elementary schools – Robert L. Vann and A. Leo Weil. Some were assigned to Herron Hill Jr. High and a few to Fifth Avenue High. All the schools mentioned had a large Black population and all were located in the Hill District. Complete data for all the years on student population are not available. However, Table 3-4 indicates the trend of Black student population in some Hill District schools in 1929.

---

18 Leo Woods and Elmo Calloway in discussions with the author, 1973
19 Waunetta Alston and Mary Louise Stone in discussions with the author, 1973.

TABLE 3-4* BLACK STUDENT POPULATION IN SELECTED SCHOOLS, 1929	
SCHOOL	**% BLACK**
Watt (R.L. Vann)	94.82
Somers	93.93
Rose	91.10
Minersville	67.84
Moorhead	57.80
Franklin	56.10

*The Social Condition of the Negro in The Hill,
Urban League of Pittsburgh, 1930, 83.

In 1942, Herron Hill Jr. High had 1396 Black students out of a total enrollment of 1672 students. Fifth Avenue Junior/Senior High had a population of 648 Blacks out of a total enrollment of 1614 students.[20] What these statistics show is that the Black teacher population in the 1940s lagged far behind the Black student population in Hill District schools.

Not all the teachers employed during the 1940s had an easy time getting employment with the School Board. Hazel Stallings had to leave Pittsburgh to teach in North Carolina in 1930 because the Board would not hire her. John Brewer, John Morton, Ruth Williams, Marion Stanton and George Poe had to prove themselves on a summer playground program before being allowed to apply as temporary substitutes. Elmo Calloway had to teach for a year in North Carolina because the Board refused to hire him. It took Leo Woods from 1940 to 1946 to finally secure a position with the Board. Frances Brown found it impossible to find a job here in 1938, so she taught in Virginia for two years and worked for the Board of Public Assistance for one year. Norine Cyrus graduated from Pitt in 1929. She went into social work because the Board was hiring no Black teachers in that year. Waunetta Alston, after graduating from Hampton Institute in Virginia in 1936, did not even bother to come back to Pittsburgh until 1946 because she

---

20 Report of the Pennsylvania State Temporary Commission on the Urban Colored Population, 1943, page. 403.

knew there were no jobs for Black teachers. One other interesting bit of discrimination was revealed during interviews conducted by the author. Some of the Black women interviewed suffered from a double form of discrimination.

At first, they were not hired because they were Black; later they were not hired because for years the Pittsburgh Board of Public Education had a prohibition against hiring married women. There was no such prohibition against hiring married men.[21]

There is a popular theory that many of the early Black teachers in the United States could be placed into distinct categories. David Tyack says that teaching was a favorite choice of careers for Black females. Others have said that most of the early Black teachers had middle-class backgrounds. Still others have indicated that they should have been largely mulattoes in keeping with the country's differential treatment of light-skinned Blacks. If these theories are true, one would expect that an examination of the early Black teacher population in Pittsburgh would reveal a group comprised mostly of light-skinned Black females from middle-class backgrounds. What the examination actually revealed was that the first Black hired by the Pittsburgh School Board in the twentieth century was a medium-brown complexioned Black. The rest of the early teachers were about evenly distributed over that range of colors commonly referred to as Black. In reference to sex, of that first group, the first hired was a man, the second a woman; the next group of six hired contained three females and three males. As nearly as can be determined, when one looks at the total number of Blacks hired in the 1940s, though there may have been more females than males, the difference is statistically insignificant and certainly nowhere near the difference one would have expected. Even though many people were happy to see Black male teachers because of the difficulties with young Black male students, this did not seriously alter the sex ratio of the first group of Blacks hired.

The question of socioeconomic class becomes far more difficult to answer. Most of the Black teachers were unwilling to discuss family background, considering the issue irrelevant to their roles in the school system. Since personnel records were unavailable it became necessary

---

21 Frank Bolden in discussion with the author, 1974.

to depend on the recollections of those interviewed. The answer depends upon the definition of "middle class." Frank Bolden said that in "those days" middle class could have meant just having a steady job. Jimmy Dean said that, in the 1920s

Black middle class people were those who "drove the rich folks' carriages." Harry Latimer indicated that middle class jobs for Blacks in the 1940s were elevator operator and bank messenger.

One measure of socioeconomic class is the occupation of one's parents. Among the positions held by the parents of the early Black teachers were: postal worker, dentist, laborer, chauffeur, foreman, physician, bank messenger, chef, teacher and mailman. Clearly, physician, teacher and dentist were middle class occupations regardless of race. Most of the other occupations were among the best jobs available to Blacks at the time, and while they may not have been middle class positions in White society, they could have been considered middle class jobs for Blacks. It is apparent that once Blacks were hired as teachers they were considered middle class, regardless of their family background.

John Brewer said that most middle class Blacks became doctors, lawyers or social workers, or they got advanced degrees and went to teach in some other city where Blacks were being hired in the school systems. He indicated that many of the first Blacks hired were men because of persistent gang problems in Pittsburgh's Hill district. Lawrence Peeler stated that most of the Blacks he saw in the early teacher population were not light-skinned, nor were they from middle class backgrounds. Paul Williams said that some were middle class but a large number were male and many were not light-skinned.

The profile of predominantly female, predominantly middle class and predominantly mulatto does not hold true for Pittsburgh. Perhaps one of the reasons for this difference is that Pittsburgh hired Black teachers much later than many other cities. It is evident that many of the people who may have fit the previously discussed profile left Pittsburgh to seek their fortunes elsewhere. Had this not taken place, the profile of the early Black teachers in Pittsburgh might have been different.

At the end of the 1940s there were approximately 50 Blacks on the Board of Education professional staff. It is not certain how many of them were full-time teachers. What is certain is that some of the Black teachers were employed in elementary schools and some in secondary schools. Some were male and some were female. Some taught English, others physical education, home economics, industrial arts and other subjects. All were assigned to teach in schools within the city's largest Black ghetto—the Hill district. It is interesting that they were all assigned to the Hill even though there were large Black settlements in Manchester, on the North Side of Pittsburgh, and Beltzhoover on the city's South Side. It is evident, at this point, that Blacks were still being discriminated against both in terms of numbers hired, subjects assigned, geographic location and level of school assignment. Most teachers were hired in subject areas deemed suitable for Blacks, i.e., physical education, home economics, and industrial arts. All were assigned to the Hill and most were assigned to elementary schools.

During the 1950s, 1960s and 1970s the number of Black teachers increased, but did not keep pace with the increasing size of the Black student population. At the beginning of the 1950s Blacks still represented a very small percentage of the professional employees of the Pittsburgh Board of Public Education. Blacks constituted two percent of the total professional staff in 1950. By the end of the 1950s Blacks would still constitute less than ten percent of the total professional staff.[22] During that same period Black student enrollment would rise to 32% of all children in the Pittsburgh public schools. The Black population in the city itself rose to 16.8%[23]. On August 26, 1950 a story appeared in *The Pittsburgh Courier* with the Headline, "4 Get Teaching Posts Outside Hill." The article went on to say, "Thus the Board of Education abandoned the policy of using Negro teachers only in Hill District schools, a practice followed since the first appointment of Negro teachers in 1936." The article named the following teachers:

> Mrs. Ethel Moore Stewart, transferred from Mckelvy to Colfax School in Squirrel Hill;

> Mrs. Sarah L. Harvey, transferred from A. Leo Weil to Crescent in Brushton;

---

22 Pittsburgh Board of Education, Office of Statistics.
23 *The Quest for Racial Equality in the Pittsburgh Public Schools*, Annual Report, 1965, page 7.

Miss Ethel West, transferred from McKelvey to Madison School; and

Mrs. Norine A. Cyrus, transferred from Weil to Madison.

In the same article, *The Pittsburgh Courier* said that there were 32 Black teachers in the Pittsburgh school system who were employed as full-time teachers and 13 employed as fulltime substitutes. In total, there were 64 Blacks employed by the Board as of the end of August 1950. At the time of these appointments in 1950, the Black populations in the three schools to receive their first Black teachers were as listed in Table 3-5.

TABLE 3-5 BLACK POPULATION IN SCHOOLS OUTSIDE OF THE HILL RECEIVING FIRST BLACK TEACHERS IN 1950		
SCHOOL	# OF STUDENTS	
	BLACK	TOTAL
Colfax	2	1,075
Crescent	318	868
Madison	496	574

While Colfax had only a token Black population, Crescent was well integrated in terms of student population and Madison was predominantly Black before the faculty was integrated. What is more interesting is that Crescent is located in what was then a neighborhood in transition—i.e., Blacks were starting to enter the neighborhood in large numbers. Madison had been a predominantly Black school for many years and, while located in the same postal zone as the Hill, was not considered as part of the Hill for many years. It was referred to as "Sugar Top" and was considered by residents and others as being more a part of Oakland than the Hill. The residents of Sugar Top, or Schenley Heights as it is formally known, were for many years the upper echelon of Pittsburgh's Black community. So, even though the school had been a "Black" school for many years, it did not get its first Black teacher until 1950.

The author talked with Norine Cyrus about Madison School. She said that she did not experience many problems while working at the school, but did think it was strange that she was the first Black teacher in the school, especially since it had been predominantly Black for years before 1950. Bee McHaffey, another teacher assigned to Madison during the 1950s, told the author that she had been substituting in the Pittsburgh school system since 1953. Even though she lived right across the street from Madison School, she was never assigned as a substitute at that school. She is certain that this was because of her race. The Board had two Black teachers at the school—Norine Cyrus and Ethel West, and apparently it was not interested in having more. All Mrs. Mahaffey's teaching assignments as a substitute were in Hill District schools. Finally, she was assigned as a teacher at Madison in 1954. She said that she did have some problems with some of the parents because of her race. She indicated that, for some reason, many of the parents (both Black and White) had the notion that their kids would get a better education if they were taught by Whites. Apparently, some had not yet been convinced that Blacks made good teachers.[24]

By 1950, the School Board had begun to place Blacks in teaching positions outside of the Hill. Still, at this time, most Blacks were being placed in elementary schools. Blacks were still being discouraged from applying for positions outside of elementary schools by their college instructors as well as by the Board of Education itself.

Herron Hill Jr. High School, which had been predominantly Black for many years by 1950, now was nearly 100 % Black in terms of student population: 1,103 Black students versus 41 White students.[25] Despite this nearly 100 % Black student body, most of the teachers were White, as were the members of the administration. The entire coaching staff for all school sports was also White.[26] Other Black people joined the staff of Herron Hill Jr. High School during the 1950s. The author talked to some of them. William Green joined the Herron Hill faculty in 1955 as a math teacher. He had been a student at Herron Hill, and when

---

24 Norine Cyrus and Bee McHaffey in discussions with the author, 1974.
25 Pittsburgh Board of Education, Office of Statistics.
26 Frank Bolden in discussion with the author, 1974.

Green returned from the service, Mr. Morgart was still the principal and asked for Green to be assigned to the school. Green had no difficulty at the school, from parents, teachers or students. He feels that this was at least in part due to his having attended the school with many of the parents and that he had been a student under some of his present peers.

Ted Vassar was assigned to Herron Hill in 1957. He, too, was treated well, as was Lois Golden, who started there in 1953. Also assigned to Herron Hill, in 1957, was Ollie Mae Guice. Herb Parrish gave up nearly $1,000 a year to join the faculty at Herron Hill. He had been a postal worker, even though he had a Master's degree, because he could not find a job as a secondary school science teacher. When asked why he was willing to give up seniority and money to teach in Herron Hill despite its reputation as a "rough ghetto school," Parrish replied that he felt there was a need for young Black males to be involved in the education of Black youngsters and he was prepared to take up that challenge. He felt that his militant personality in the defense of Black children cost him much in terms of his personal advancement in the system. Parrish became highly respected by his peers and parents. Students came to both respect and admire him. The author recalls that occasionally some student with a reputation would attempt to physically fight Parrish. These challenges soon stopped when it was clear that Parrish was both intelligent and physically tough.

Many common threads run through all the interviews with Blacks who taught at Herron Hill during the 1940s and 1950s. All said that they got along well with the White faculty members and that there was little friction. All felt that Mr. John Morgart, who was principal there for many years, was a man "ahead of his time." He had involved the community in the affairs of the school many years before the concept of community involvement became popular. Perhaps this community involvement was one of the clues to the harmony between the White faculty members and the Black faculty and students. It appears as if the Black community exercised a great deal of influence over the affairs of the school and, in a sense, "rode herd" over what transpired. All the Blacks interviewed looked back on Herron Hill as one of their finest and most meaningful experiences.

While some headway was being made by Blacks during this time in securing positions in secondary schools, many people interviewed by the author' spoke of being dissuaded from seeking teaching positions in high schools. Herb Parrish recalled that his teachers and advisors at the University of

Pittsburgh tried to get him to take up elementary education because he stood a better chance of getting a job in an elementary school. Ernest Huddle could not get a position in the high schools, so he worked in the steel mills and the postal service until 1959. According to Mr. Huddle, in 1951 his advisor at Pitt asked him what he planned to do after graduation. Huddle's reply was that he planned on teaching high school. His advisor's next question was, "Where do you plan to go?" When Huddle said he was planning on staying here, the advisor suggested that Huddle might have to go elsewhere, because of the racial prejudice in Pittsburgh.[27]

Mr. Robert Cook told the author that he had been trying to break into teaching in secondary schools since 1946, but was unable to do so. Instead, he went to work for the Board of Public Assistance. He decided later that he probably would be able to get into the system more easily as a school social worker. He was successful in this attempt, but said that in some schools he had no office and no place to work. He was told that he was not to make waves but simply "do his job." Mr. Cook was able to break into secondary education as a teacher, finally, in 1957.

In 1959, Ollie Mae Guice had tried to get into the school system as a teacher in secondary education. She was told by the personnel director at the Board of Education that there were no positions for Blacks in secondary education. Maxine Whedbee taught Spanish in Louisville, Kentucky, from 1934 to 1954. She taught in Washington, D.C., from 1929 to 1934. Mrs. Guice left the city because she was told at Pitt that she would never get a job teaching in Pittsburgh, let alone teaching Spanish on the secondary level. Audia Mae Gilliard had a difficult time getting into high school teaching because of her race. She said the main problem was the policy of the Board. When she asked about teaching on the high school level, she was told by the Board's personnel director that the high schools were not ready for "her kind" (meaning Black).[28]

Alice Bernice Wade said that this same personnel director (Mr. Roberts) told her in 1947 that she should go back to school to get

27 Herb Parrish and Ernest Huddle in discussions with the author, 1973.
28 Ollie Mae Guice and Audia Mae Gilliard in discussions with the author, 1973.

certification to teach elementary school because the Board "can't put Blacks in high school." Mrs. Wade's sister did, in fact, return to school and take elementary education classes. Alice Wade did not. She said it was not uncommon during the 1940s and 1950s for the personnel manager at the Board to try to force Blacks to re-educate themselves in elementary education. Mary Louise Stone was refused a job as a home economics teacher in Pittsburgh high schools. Instead, she was allowed to substitute, without proper certification, in elementary schools.

The Board forced her to re-educate herself in elementary education before she could secure a full-time position. Mrs. Stone became certified and received her Master's degree in elementary education. Still wanting to teach home economics, as soon as she was hired by the Board she indicated she wanted to become a full-time substitute teacher in home economics.[29]

Fifth Avenue High School, which had become integrated in the 1940s, continued to get a trickle of Blacks as teachers. It should be remembered that Fifth Avenue had been a predominantly Black school since 1947.[30] Table 3-6 lists the Black student population at Fifth Avenue during the 1950s.

---

29 Allice Bernice Wade and Mary Louise Stone in discussions with the author, 1976.

30 *The Pittsburgh Press*, Roto Section, June 6, 1976.

TABLE 3-6 STUDENT POPULATION AT FIFTH AVENUE HIGH SCHOOL BY YEAR AND RACE		
YEAR	**STUDENT POPULATION**	
	BLACK	**WHITE**
1950	967	434
1951	1,032	414
1952	1,046	335
1953	1,044	299
1954	955	319
1955	975	308
1956	1,053	202
1957	1,016	174
1958	956	97
1959	828	127

In spite of the serious gang problems that John Brewer talked about, it was not until 1955 that the first Black male teacher was hired at Fifth Avenue. He was William Fisher, who spent thirteen years at the school—eleven as a teacher and two as the principal. He recalls that he was treated "royally" by all the people. He suspects that "some folks" were happy to see him because they didn't want to have to deal with the young Black males at the school. The second Black male hired at the school was Irv Biggs. Biggs said he and Fisher were put into rooms that were side by side. "Probably," he said, "because they were hoping that the niggers would kill each other off." Mr. Biggs ran into some racism at Fifth Avenue—some kinds more subtle than others. He felt that the White principal was ineffective because he was "petrified by Blacks."[31]

Another of the early Black teachers hired in 1955 to teach at Fifth Avenue, was Bob Munjin. He, too, says he was treated "pretty well" by all concerned. Nan Currington, who was hired in 1950 to teach at Fifth Avenue, said that although she was treated well she felt that Black teachers "had to be perfect." They were expected to dress better, exhibit

---

31 William Fisher and Irv Briggs in discussions with the author, 1976.

better manners and be better teachers than Whites. Also hired in 1950 was Helen Faison, who said she, too, had no problems at Fifth Avenue, but she had not been able to get a job in 1946, when she had applied for a position as a high school teacher.[32]

Alice Bernice Wade also began teaching at Fifth Avenue in 1950. Mrs. Wade, who retired from teaching in 1966, tells a different story about teaching at Fifth Avenue. "It was horrible. White teachers would not sit with the Blacks in the lunch room or they would turn their backs when we entered the room. An old White English teacher, Mrs. Dimling, said to me when I first came to the school, 'How can you be teaching; we don't have Blacks teaching English'." (Mrs. Wade was the second Black English teacher in the city. She would have been the first had she not been ill. As it was, Mildred Keith, who taught at Herron Hill, became the first.)[33]

Continuing her description of what it was like at Fifth Avenue in those days, Mrs. Wade said that the principal was patronizing and gave Black teachers heavier teaching loads and all the students with discipline problems. She related an incident in which she protested at a meeting about the portrayal of Blacks in a Pittsburgh teachers' magazine. It seems that every month a cartoon about Blacks appeared in this magazine. It was always about Fifth Avenue Black students and was always unflattering, being complete with the characters speaking in alleged Black dialect. When she protested that the cartoons were derogatory, one of the Black male teachers said he thought the jokes were funny. Mrs. Wade accused this man of being nothing short of an Uncle Tom. On another occasion she said that a White teacher walked up to this same Black man and said, "You have such a beautiful ebony face and your eyes and teeth are so white." Mrs. Wade said that, instead of being angry, the Black man smiled. While teaching at Fifth Avenue, she often saw the police take Black kids out in the alley and beat them, because they had misbehaved in school. She is sure that the administration knew what would happen to a Black youngster if they (the administration) called the police in on a discipline problem. Despite this knowledge, the administration did nothing to change the situation.

---

32 Bob Munjin, Nan Currington, and Helen Faison in discussions with the author, 1973.
33 Alice Bernice Wade in discussion with the author, 1973.

One day she took over a class for a White teacher who was absent. She looked in the teacher's attendance book and found an "N" or a "W" after each of the names. Each student with an "N" after his or her name had no grades higher than Cs, Ds or Fs. All the students with "W" after their names had only grades of B or A. Mrs. Wade said it did not take long for her to figure out that "N" meant "nigger" or Negro and "W" meant White.

Mrs. Wade also had some strong opinions about the Board of Education. She said that they were insensitive to Blacks, tried to make Blacks re-educate themselves in elementary education in order to get jobs, and constantly passed over Blacks for principalships. She said "the only time the Board started even considering promoting Blacks to spots as principals was after the riots." Mrs. Wade related how she had always been in trouble because she was so vocal. "I have to have dignity. No one robs me of that. My mind, to me, my kingdom is. I ain't going to keep my mouth shut. You must not let anyone buy you." When asked how she could explain the difference between her impressions about teaching at Fifth Avenue in the 1950s and some other accounts, she said, "Some Blacks were not too much in favor of other Blacks and some were just short-sighted. Others saw the problems but just didn't push."

Ernestine Parks began her teaching career at Fifth Avenue in 1955 in physical education. She said most of the White teachers were reluctant to take up with Black teachers. "They would turn their back on you, or look the other way when they saw you coming." She related that she did not socialize with the White teachers or go to their parties because of the way they treated Black students. Mrs. Parks recalled that when she was teaching she was upset with some of her fellow Black workers because "they were cowards and would not stand up to the White teachers."[34]

Schenley High School had long had a reputation for being a fine school, but it, too, like most other schools with large Black student populations, was controlled by Whites. During the 1950s, most of the faculty and administration were White. It was not until 1954 that the first Black teacher in Schenley was hired. The story made headlines in

---

34 Ernestine Parks in discussion with the author, 1973.

the January 30,1954 edition of *The Pittsburgh Courier*. The headline read, "Schenley to Have First Negro Teacher." The article said that Jody Harris would be the first Black teacher ever to teach at Schenley High School. He would also be the first Black ever to teach industrial arts at the high school level.

In order to put the hiring of Black teachers at Schenley High School into the proper perspective during the 1950s, it is necessary to examine the growth of the Black student population from 1950 to 1959. The following are those attendance figures.

TABLE 3-7* TEACHER AND STUDENT POPULATION AT SCHENLEY HIGH SCHOOL BY YEAR AND RACE			
	POPULATION		
YEAR	BLACK TEACHERS	BLACK STUDENTS	WHITE STUDENTS
1950	0	658	1,120
1951	0	659	1,127
1952	0	681	1,010
1953	0	717	984
1954	1	709	986
1955	2	723	921
1956	4	740	879
1957	5	774	917
1958	5	795	868
1959	5	736	756
*Pittsburgh Board of Education, Office of Statistics.			

The data show that Schenley High School had a sizeable Black enrollment during the decade of the 1950s. By 1959, the school was nearly 50% Black, yet the school's proportion of Black teachers was much lower. An interesting aspect of the change in student population at Schenley during the 1950s is not so much the rise in Black population, which was not dramatic, but rather the dramatic drop in White student population. Either Whites were moving away from the area or they sent their children to other schools. Actually, both things were happening.

The author interviewed some of the early Black teachers at Schenley High School, including Jody Harris. He was offered a principalship in 1955, but declined because he felt that the Board was trying to get him into the elementary school so that he would be out of the way when it came time to appoint a new principal at the predominantly Black Herron Hill Junior High. Mr. Harris said that he was treated very well at Schenley.[35]

Also among the Black teachers entering Schenley during the 1950s was Audia Mae Gilliard, who was in the home economics area and who said things were pretty good at Schenley. She said standards for the students were much higher and that she had more materials to work with because "you get more things when a school was mixed." Alice Bernice Wade also went to Schenley during this time, as an English teacher. She stated that they had a classier kind of bigot at Schenley than had been at Fifth Avenue. "They would speak but wouldn't associate with you," she said. She also recalled that there were no Black clerks in the front office when she got to Schenley. Once, when she asked a White English teacher for a report that was to be given to Mrs. Wade, the White teacher went into a tirade and said, "I can't help it if these children are stupid. I taught their parents and they were stupid, too." This tirade took place in the hallway, where everyone on the floor could hear it. As had been the case at Fifth Avenue, Mrs. Wade said that the Black teachers got the heaviest loads, the worst students, and the discipline problems.[36]

Also among the teachers hired to teach at Schenley during this period was Elmo C. Calloway, who was appointed in 1955 as a math teacher. He said some of the White teachers were a bit standoffish, but all in all he experienced no racial problems. Robert Cook was assigned as a social studies teacher in 1957. He, like Mr. Calloway, experienced no difficulties as a result of his race.[37]

Other schools were getting their first Black teachers during the 1950s. Dorothea Peeler (sister of Lawrence Peeler, the first Black teacher hired by the Board in the 20th century) was the first Black teacher at Gladstone Jr. High School in 1953. At the time, Gladstone had 123 Black students and 396 White students.[38] Ms. Peeler said that,

35　Jody Harris in discussion with the author, 1975.

36　Audia Mae Gilliard and Alice Bernice Wade in discussions with the author, 1973.

37　Robert Cook and Elmo C. Calloway in discussions with the author, 1973.

38　Pittsburgh Board of Education, Office of Statistics.

before her assignment at Gladstone, she was told that she would be the first Black at the school. Some of the older White women at Gladstone did not want to speak to her; other teachers were nice. Some of the teachers needled her about the behavior of "her" Black kids. One White teacher said, in Ms. Peeler's presence, that she didn't want to work with a nigger. Parents and students, however, presented no problems based on her race.[39]

Ollie Mae Guice was the first Black to be assigned to Westinghouse High School. Her date of appointment was 1952. Table 3-8 lists the Black student population at Westinghouse High School during the 1950s.

TABLE 3-8* STUDENT POPULATION AT WESTINGHOUSE HIGH SCHOOL BY YEAR AND RACE		
YEAR	**STUDENT POPULATION**	
	BLACK	**WHITE**
1950	682	1,118
1951	631	1,118
1952	670	965
1953	660	947
1954	754	908
1955	897	781
1956	1,444	918
1957	1,612	685
1958	1,798	629
1959	1,784	439
*Pittsburgh Board of Education, Office of Statistics		

Thus, in the year Ms. Guice was appointed, the Black population of Westinghouse was 670, as contrasted with 965 Whites, or about 41% Black. Yet, the first Black teacher hirings lagged far behind the growth of the Black student population.

---

39 Dorothea Peeler in discussion with author, 1976.

In viewing the statistics about the changing student population of Westinghouse, two trends are evident. First, there was a dramatic increase in the number of Black students, from 682 Black students in 1950 to 1,784 in 1959. The second dramatic change was a decrease in the number of White students attending the school, from 1,118 in 1950 to 439 in 1959. These shifts in racial composition occurred during this time because of the redevelopment of the Hill District. Even though the city fathers claimed that they were going to redevelop the Hill in such a way that would allow the previous residents to return, such was not the case. The dwelling units built—the Chatham Center Hotel and the Washington Plaza Apartments—were far too expensive for the previous residents of the Hill, whether they were Black or White.

Homewood at this time had a small, primarily middle-class Black population. When Blacks were forced out of the Hill redevelopment area, many of them sought homes in the Homewood-Brushton area.

Some Blacks who owned homes in the area subdivided their houses and rented rooms and apartments to the newcomers. Other Blacks gained access as unscrupulous realtors moved into the area and engaged in the practice of "blockbusting," or scaring Whites into selling their property cheaply by telling them that Blacks were going to take over the area. Once the Whites moved, the homes were sold at much inflated prices to Blacks, or were subdivided and rented to Blacks at exorbitant rates.[40] Consequently, Whites left the area rapidly and Blacks moved in to take their place. By 1959, Homewood was a predominantly Black area. That shift was reflected in the student population and became a factor in the Pittsburgh Board of Education's hiring more Black teachers for Westinghouse High School. Nevertheless, as was usually the case, student integration ran well ahead of faculty integration.

In an interview with the author, Ms. Guice said she experienced no difficulty at Westinghouse because of her race. Another of the early Blacks at Westinghouse was Herman McClain, who came to Westinghouse in 1955 as an English teacher. Mr. McClain said he was assigned at the same time as Mildred Glenn and another Black person, so he assumes that they all share the honor of being the "second" Black teacher assigned to Westinghouse. McClain described the way he was

40 Herb Wilkerson and Alma Fox in discussions with the author, 1975.

treated by the White faculty as "extremes." Some treated him extremely well; some were extremely uncooperative. He also feels strongly that he was purposely passed over, because of his race, when the chairman of the English department left in 1964 or 1965. The job should have been his; instead, it went to a less experienced White teacher. Ernest Huddle followed McClain to Westinghouse in 1959, as a social studies teacher. Except for one teacher who got upset when he moved next door to her, Huddle was treated very well by the other Whites on the staff.[41]

In 1956, when Charles B. McNutt was hired as the first Black teacher at Oliver High School, the Black population at that school was 300 out of 1527 students. Mr. McNutt experienced no racial problems. In that same year, the Black population at Peabody High School was 236 of 1,719 students.[42] It was at this time that Paul Williams was assigned as the first Black teacher at Peabody. He recalls being treated well by the faculty, staff and students.[43]

The Pittsburgh Branch of the NAACP was interested in the employment of Black teachers and was apparently dealing with the Board of Education, not so much as relates to the hiring of additional Black teachers, as much as non-discriminatory placement of Black teachers who had already been hired. In a memo to the Chairman of the Education Committee of the Pennsylvania State Conference of Branches of the NAACP, written in 1958, Marian Jordan, then Executive Secretary of the Pittsburgh Branch of the NAACP, said, "In response to your question as to whether schools in this area are integrated, we do have integrated faculties. However, our branch has impressed the school board with the need for a wider distribution of Negro teachers. The pattern has been to place a majority of Negro teachers in predominantly Negro schools." In response to the question of whether prepared teachers in Pittsburgh had been refused employment because of race, Mrs. Jordan replied, "In the past there have been allegations of discrimination based on race. We have had no specific complaints in this area during the past year.[44]

---

41 Ollie Mae Guice and Herman McClain in discussions with the author, 1973.
42 Pittsburgh Board of Education, Office of Statistics.
43 Paul Williams in discussion with the author, 1973.
44 Marion Jordan, Memo dated September 12, 1958. Archives of the Industrial Society, University of Pittsburgh, Hillman Library.

By 1960, most of the schools in the City of Pittsburgh still had all-White faculties and staffs. According to Board of Education Office of Student Attendance, the following schools were integrated:

GRADE LEVEL	TOTAL # SCHOOLS	# SCHOOLS WITH 1 OR MORE	
		BLACK STUDENTS	BLACK TEACHERS
Elementary	88	55	23
Secondary	25	22	8
Provided by the Office of Student Attendance, Pittsburgh Board of Education			

During this time, the School Board continued the pattern of discrimination which assigns teachers by race – Black teachers by and large to Black or nearly all-Black schools, and White teachers to White or mixed schools, as illustrated in Table 3-9.

TABLE 3-9* PROPORTION OF BLACK TEACHERS BY PERCENT OF BLACK ENROLLMENT & SCHOOL LEVEL, OCTOBER 1963**		
% BLACK ENROLLMENT	ELEMENTARY	SECONDARY
<5%	3.8	7.7
<25%	4.4	18.9
>25%	95.6	81.0
*The Status of Education of Negroes in Pittsburgh, 1963-1964, Pittsburgh Commission on Human Relations, p. 17. **Excludes teachers in special and vocational schools.		

**Herron Hill Junior High School Students
receiving award from principal**

**Children with Student Crossing Guard,
A Leo Weil School on left in background**

Students at Madison School

Students in front of Schenley High School

First grade students on first day of school at Crescent School

**Mothers and children on first day of school
at Baxter Elementary School**

Children in front of Pittsburgh Public School #3

Students at Westinghouse High School

Political Pressure Mounts

In the 1960s, as the country turned more and more to the issue of racial equality, pressure on the Pittsburgh Board of Public Education mounted as various groups interested in Black equality turned their attention to the Board. The Urban League of Pittsburgh, in October 1965, expressed its concern over the plight of Black teachers in the Public School system. In a report, the League accused the Board of selecting the "best" Black teachers and using them to integrate previously White schools. The report went on to indicate that "one half [55] of the public schools still have all-White faculties, while there are at least seven schools with a 40% or more Negro faculty. One school [Miller] has a predominantly Negro faculty."[45]

External pressure on the Board was not only coming from the Urban League. Pressure was also being applied by the NAACP, the Congress of Racial Equality, and the United Negro Protest Committee. The Board was the target of many civil rights demonstrations during this period, as indicated in a 1966 NAACP press release which said a demonstration would take place November 22, 1967, "to demonstrate the community's dissatisfaction concerning the school administrations' and the Board of Education's failure to take adequate immediate action for racial integration of pupils and faculties in the Pittsburgh schools."[46] Many times during the 1960s, pickets ringed the administration building of the Board of Education on Bellefield Street.

Often during this period, Blacks and Whites participated in stormy meetings with the Board over teacher and student integration. Parents and civil rights groups acted against individual teachers and principals who were considered by Blacks to be insensitive and even dangerous when dealing with Blacks. Angry Black parents from Esplen, Broadhead Manor, Arlington Heights, Northview Heights, East Liberty, Garfield, Northside, the Hill, and other areas stormed Board meetings protesting the racist and discriminatory practices of the Board. Herb Wilkerson and Alma Fox, both of whom were past Executive Secretaries of the Pittsburgh NAACP, recalled that there were several negotiating sessions between the NAACP and the Board relative to discrimination. Both

---

45 Urban League of Pittsburgh, untitled document dated October 19, 1965, NAACP files, Archives of the Industrial Society, University of Pittsburgh, Hillman Library, page. 13.
46 NAACP press release, November 9, 1966, University of Pittsburgh, Hillman Library.

agreed that most of the emphasis was on teacher and pupil integration rather than on the hiring of more teachers.[47]

Although, in the minds of many, the progress of Blacks in the public school system of Pittsburgh was painfully slow, Blacks were making some progress. Black teachers continued to integrate previously all-White faculties. One of those teachers was Dorothea Peeler, who had integrated the faculty of Gladstone Jr. High in 1953. In 1963, Ms. Peeler integrated the faculty at South Hills High School. She says she was treated pretty well, but felt that she could make a greater contribution in a Black school. Consequently, in 1966 she asked to be transferred to Westinghouse High School to, as she put it, "replace one of those White teachers who think Blacks can't learn."[48] At the time she integrated the South Hills faculty, there were 162 Blacks in a total student enrollment of 1,980.[49]

In the same year, John Young became the first Black at Prospect Jr. High School in Mount Washington. Blacks at this time formed only 3.2% of the student population, or 22 out of 684 students. In 1969, he became the first Black activities director at Perry High School on the North Side. According to the Pittsburgh Board of Education statistics, Perry had little more than token integration, having 190 Black students and 1,318 White students. The first Black teacher at Perry was Charles McNutt, who was appointed in 1964.

By 1969, Blacks were making progress toward some measure of equality in numbers of Black teachers hired. Much of the progress is attributed to several factors. First, the 1960s was a period of heightened consciousness about the racial discrimination practiced against Blacks by this society. It is certain that some people on the Board of Education were affected by this temporary mood of wanting to correct the racial ills of the society. Second, there was internal pressure on the Board because more Black teachers were staying in Pittsburgh than previously. These teachers exerted pressure on the Board by applying for teaching positions in Pittsburgh rather than seeking positions in other cities. Furthermore, Blacks during this period and into the 1970s were far less likely to accept the Board's not hiring them without putting up some protest, either through the Black media, the civil rights organizations,

---

47 Herb Wilkerson and Alma Fox in discussions with the author, 1977.
48 Dorothea Peeler in discussion with the author, 1973.
49 Pittsburgh Board of Education, Office of Statistics.

the federal government and/or the Mayor's Commission on Human Relations.[50] As will be discussed later, many Blacks would feel that this climate changed during the 1970s.

Also during the 1960s Presidents Kennedy and Johnson made the rights of Blacks a federal issue, and pumped millions of dollars into programs of compensatory education and other programs which had direct impact on the Pittsburgh Public School system. In order to receive these monies, school systems had to hire on a non-discriminatory basis. In addition, the School Board had to have the support of Black citizens in order not to have their funding cut off. The Board was aware of this and the author can recall that the Board sent Black representatives to local Office of Economic Opportunity (OEO) Board of Directors to elicit their support for various programs.[51] So, beyond the pressure being applied to educational institutions by civil rights-oriented organizations, the Department of Health, Education and Welfare and the Equal Employment Opportunity Commission were actively involved in seeing that Blacks received equal opportunities in this area.[52]

External pressure was also being brought to bear through the media. *The Pittsburgh Courier* continued its crusade for equality. Black radio shows on WAMO radio talked about the problems Blacks were having with the Board of Education. During this time, Black-oriented television programs first appeared. On the national level there was Black Journal. On the local level, the first Black-produced television show was Black Horizons (produced and hosted by the author) on WQED in 1968, followed by other, similar programs on the commercial stations. These shows addressed themselves to the issue of Black employment in the Pittsburgh Public School system on many occasions. The members of the Board, as well as Board administrators, frequently found themselves on these shows being bombarded with questions from Black hosts and program guests.[53]

Parents and citizens' groups also provided additional pressure as they picketed, stormed meetings, disrupted Board meetings and waged

---

50 Herb Wilkerson and Alma Fox in discussions with the author, 1976.
51 David Epperson, Past Executive Director, Pittsburgh Poverty Program in discussion with the author, 1978.
52 Interviews with various civil rights leaders and EEOC officers, 1973-1978.
53 Ralph Proctor, personal observations as first producer/host of Black Horizons and a member of the National Organization of Black Media Producers.

an intensive campaign against the Board over the issues of Black employment, teacher assignment, racism and student and teacher agreement. This pressure was exerted through groups from nearly every Black neighborhood in the Pittsburgh area. Most of them were organized with the assistance of OEO workers from the community organization components of anti-poverty offices.

It is important not to overlook the internal pressure being applied to the Board of Education. It was during this period that the first Black was elected to the presidency of the Pittsburgh Board of Education – Gladys McNairy, who was elected to the Board in 1964 and became the President in 1971. Mrs. McNairy applied much pressure to members of the Board in order to get them to address the needs of Black students and teachers. She was able to get some of the White Board members to understand the problems of Blacks and to realize that the Board had indeed discriminated against Blacks.[54] Internal pressure also came from Black teachers who were already employed by the Pittsburgh school system. They constantly provided civil rights groups with inside information, pressured the Board for their own promotions and in other ways kept the heat on the Board.[55]

By 1969, there were 407 Black teachers and 2,820 White teachers employed by the public schools. Blacks now represented 14.5% of the teacher population.[56] In that same year, the Black student population had grown to approximately 41% of the total student population in the public schools—28,849 Blacks vs. 70,199 Whites.[57] It is evident that student integration had far outstripped teacher integration.

As Pittsburgh entered the 1970s, Black teachers were being employed in larger numbers, but the Board of Education still practiced racial discrimination in the form of failure to integrate the faculties at many schools. By 1973, the data show that, of the 87 elementary schools operated by the Board of Education, 42 or 43.8% of them had no Black teachers (see Table 3-5). Of these 42 schools, three (Chartiers, Clayton and Friendship) were predominantly Black. Three others (Fineview, Regent Square and Spring Hill) were nearly 50% Black. All

---

54 Gladys McNairy in discussion with the author, 1978.
55 Various teachers and civil rights leaders in discussion with the author, 1973-1978.
56 "Report of Racial Census of Staff," Pittsburgh Board of Public Education, 1974, pags 1-4.
57 Pittsburgh Board of Education, Office of Statistics.

of the schools on the secondary level had at least one Black teacher. However, of the special schools operated by the Board as of 1973, seven employed no Blacks. Those seven were: Downtown Opportunity, South Vocational, Adult Basic Education Learning Center, Goodwill Industries, Home for Crippled Children, YIKC (East Liberty) and Pressley Ridge (see Table 3-10).

TABLE 3-10*
PITTSBURGH ELEMENTARY & SPECIAL PURPOSE SCHOOLS WITH NO BLACK TEACHERS AS OF 1973 COMPARISON OF WHITE TEACHERS AND STUDENT POPULATION BY RACE

ELEMENTARY SCHOOL	WHITE TEACHERS	STUDENTS	
		BLACK	WHITE
Banksville	17	11	407
Beechwood	36	47	820
Bon-Air	5	2	129
Brookline	35	11	993
Carmalt	7	2	117
Chartiers	11	187	98
Chatham	13	45	353
Clayton	23	259	253
Concord	14	0	429
East Park	10	49	167
East Street	9	12	133
Fairview	8	0	183
Fineview	11	124	181
Friendship	17	199	137
Fulton	27	77	500
Grandview	18	8	532
Halls Grove	6	55	102
Hays	7	48	139
Knoxville	15	147	362
Lee	11	2	324
Linden	20	142	384

Mifflin	16	34	741
Morningside	17	22	432
Morse	8	39	229
McCleary	14	9	230
Overbrook	22	96	501
Park Place	10	53	122
Phillips	14	47	428
Prospect	20	28	463
Regent Square	9	78	89
Quentin Roosevelt	12	1	281
Schaeffer	10	3	257
Sheraden	30	28	835
Spring Garden	13	33	233
Spring Hill	11	109	158
Sterrett	14	91	140
Swisshelm	7	28	114
West Liberty	22	3	519
West Wood	20	57	462
Whittier	18	20	391
Wightman	22	85	420
Woolslair	19	78	259
Special Purpose			
Downtown Opportunity	2	17	13
South Vocational	11	14	37
Adult Basic Education Learning Center	3	16	10
Goodwill Industry	4	5	7
Home for Crippled Children	2	Data not available	
YIKC (East Liberty)	6		
Pressley Ridge	2	4	16
* "Report of Staff Racial Census," Pittsburgh Board of Education, 1974, pages 1-4.			

While there were some schools which had no Black teachers assigned, there were other schools which had only token integration of faculties, with from one to three Black teachers employed. Those schools are listed in Table 3-ll.

TABLE 3-11* **PITTSBURGH PUBLIC SCHOOLS** **WITH 1-3 BLACK TEACHERS, 1973**		
SCHOOL	**# TEACHERS**	
ELEMENTARY	**BLACK**	**WHITE**
Burgwin	1	28
Colfax	1	26
Conley	2	23
Davis	1	6
Dillworth	1	18
East Hills (Primary)	2**	5
Fairywood	3	16
Gladstone	1	15
Holmes	1	22
Liberty	3	20
Lincoln	3	19
Horace Mann	1	13
Minadeo	1	26
Morrow	1	18
Mt. Oliver	1	19
McNaugher	2	31
Rogers	3	25
Schaller	1	16
Stevens	1	29
Sunnyside	2	21
Secondary		
Allegheny	3	46
Conroy Jr. High	1	22
Greenfield Jr. High	1	12

Mifflin Jr. High	1	10
Perry	3	63
Prospect Jr. High	2	35
South	2	70
Special Purpose		
Educational Medical	1	5
North Side Opportunity	1**	2
East Liberty Opportunity	2**	4
Washington Ed Center	1	8
Connelley Vocational	1	30
Pioneer Elementary	1	22

*"Report of Staff Racial Census," Pittsburgh Board of Education, 1974, pages 1-4.
**Because the overall faculty in these schools is so small,
this cannot be considered token integration.

This clearly shows that, of the 21 secondary schools operated by the Board in 1973, seven of them employed three or fewer Black teachers. In fact, as Table 3-12 will show, a case can be made for the argument that 19 of them – all but Westinghouse and Fifth Avenue – had faculties that were integrated only on a token basis. Table 3-11 also shows that, of the 13 "special schools" operated by the Board, 11 were either not integrated or were integrated only on a token basis. Special schools were those operated for "problem" students – those with behavior problems, slow learning ability or pregnant school-age girls.

TABLE 3-12* COMPOSITION OF TEACHING PERSONNEL BY SECONDARY SCHOOLS AND RACE, 1973*			
SCHOOL	WHITE	BLACK	TOTAL
Allderdice	128	7	135
Allegheny	46	3	49
Carrick	78	4	82
Columbus Middle	32	4	36
Conroy Jr. High	22	1	23
Fifth Avenue	41	22	63
Gladstone	39	8	47
Greenfield Jr. High	12	1	13
Herron Hill Jr. High	37	8	45
Knoxville Jr. High	35	5	40
Langley	75	7	82
Latimer Jr. High	40	4	44
Mifflin Jr. High	10	1	11
Oliver	42	9	51
Peabody	110	4	114
Perry	63	3	66
Prospect	35	2	37
Schenley	63	12	75
South	70	2	72
South Hills	97	6	103
Westinghouse	90	36	126
Total			

*"Report of Staff Racial Census," Pittsburgh Board of Education, 1974, 1-4.

Table 3-12 lists all the secondary schools operated by the Board in 1973, and gives the racial composition of the teaching staff. This shows that all of the secondary schools had more White teachers than Black, and that 19 of the 21 secondary schools had only token integration of faculties. However, of the 21 schools, seven had predominantly Black student enrollments, as listed below.

TABLE 3-13*
BLACK SECONDARY SCHOOLS WITH PREDOMINANTLY BLACK STUDENT POPULATIONS, 1973

SCHOOL	BLACK STUDENTS	WHITE STUDENTS
Arsenal Girls' School	431	378
Gladstone	346	283
Fifth Avenue	900	5
Herron Hill Jr. High	417	1
Latimer Jr. High	339	60
Schenley	1,174	294
Westinghouse	2,163	2

*"Report of Staff Racial Census," Pittsburgh Board of Education, 1974, pages 1-4.

Table 3-14 lists the total teaching staff of the Board's special schools. It shows that, of the thirteen special schools operated by the Board of Public Education as of 1973, four were integrated on a token basis and seven were not integrated at all. Only the North Side Opportunity (two Whites, one Black) and the East Liberty Opportunity (four Whites, two Blacks) can be said to have been integrated on a more than token basis.

TABLE 3-14*
COMPOSITION OF TEACHING PERSONNEL IN SPECIAL SCHOOLS BY SCHOOL AND RACE, 1973

SCHOOL	WHITE	BLACK	TOTAL
Educational Medical	5	1	6
North Side Opportunity	2	1	3
East Liberty Opportunity	4	2	6
Downtown Opportunity	2	0	2
South Vocational	11	0	11
Washington Ed. Center	8	1	9
Connelley Vocational	30	1	31
Adult Basic Education Learning Center	3	0	3
Goodwill Industries	4	0	4

Pioneer Elementary	22	1	23
Home for Crippled Children	2	0	2
YIKC (East Liberty)	6	0	6
Pressley Ridge	2	0	2

*"Report of Staff Racial Census," Pittsburgh Board of Education, 1974, 1-4.

Table 3-15 shows the number of Black and White teachers in all of the elementary schools operated by the Board during 1973. These data show that, of the 87 elementary schools operated at that time, the majority either were not integrated (42 schools) or were integrated on a token basis (29 schools). Eighty-six of the 87 elementary schools had more White than Black teachers. No elementary school had more Black than White teachers, and only Vann School had as many Blacks as whites on the faculty (13 of each).

TABLE 3-15*
COMPOSITION OF TEACHING PERSONNEL
BY ELEMENTARY SCHOOL AND RACE, 1973

SCHOOL	WHITE	BLACK	TOTAL
Alington**	35	4	39
Arsenal	17	4	21
Banksville	17	0	17
Baxter	29	19	48
Beechwood	36	0	36
Belmar	23	11	34
Beltzhoover	24	6	30
Boggs	12	2	14
Bon Air	5	0	5
Brookline	35	0	35
Burgwin	28	1	29
Carmalt	7	0	7
Chartiers	11	0	11
Chatham	13	0	13
Clayton	23	0	23
Colfax	26	1	27

Concord	14	0	14
Conroy	11	7	18
Corpus Christi (East Hills)	5	4	9
Cowley	23	2	25
Crescent	25	11	36
Davis	6	1	7
Dillworth	18	1	19
East Hills (Primary)	5	2	7
East Park	10	0	10
East Street	9	0	9
Fairview	8	0	8
Fairywood	16	3	19
Fineview	11	0	11
Forbes	14	6	20
Fort Pitt	26	8	34
Frick**	38	12	50
Friendship	17	0	17
Fulton	27	0	27
Gladstone	15	1	16
Grandview	18	0	18
Greenfield	20	1	21
Halls Grove	6	0	6
Hays	7	0	7
Holmes	22	1	23
Homewood	16	8	24
Knoxville	15	0	15
Larimer**	24	9	33
Lee	11	0	11
Lemington	23	12	35
Letsche	7	6	13
Liberty	20	3	23
Lincoln	19	3	22
Linden	20	0	20

Madison	16	5	21
Manchester	23	10	33
Horace Mann	13	1	14
Mifflin	16	0	16
Miller	11	10	21
Minadeo	26	1	27
Morningside	17	0	17
Morrow	18	1	19
Morse	8	0	8
Mt. Oliver	19	1	20
P. Murray	29	4	33
McCleary	14	0	14
McKelvy	14	10	24
McNaugher	31	2	33
Northview	37	11	48
Overbrook	22	0	22
Park Place	10	0	10
Phillips	14	0	14
Prospect	20	0	20
Regent Square	9	0	9
Rogers	25	3	28
Quentin Roosevelt	12	0	12
Schaeffer	10	0	10
Schiller	16	1	17
Sheraden	30	0	30
Spring Garden	13	0	13
Spring Hill	11	0	11
Sterrett	14	0	14
Stevens	29	1	30
Sunnyside	21	2	23
Swisshelm	7	0	7
Vann	13	13	26
Weil	28	8	36

West Liberty	22	0	22
Westwood	20	0	20
Whittier	18	0	18
Wightman	22	0	22
Woolslair	19	0	19

*"Report of Staff Racial Census," Pittsburgh Board of Education, 1974, 1-4.
**Total includes teaching interns.

The total number of Black and White teachers in the public school system, as of 1973, is listed below:

TABLE 3-16*			
TEACHER POPULATION IN PITTSBURGH BY TYPE OF SCHOOL AND RACE, 1973			
TYPE	**WHITE**	**BLACK**	**TOTAL**
Elementary	1,564	233	1,797
Secondary	1,165	149	1,314
Special	101	7	108
Total	2,830	389	3,219

*"Report of Staff Racial Census," Pittsburgh Board of Education, 1974, pages 1-4.

By this time, Blacks also held 34 of 98 principal positions, 25 of 71 vice-principal positions, 28 of 101 counselor positions, 8 of 47 supervisor/coordinator positions, and 2 of 6 nurse/social worker positions.

Under the external and internal pressures previously mentioned, the Pittsburgh Board of Education hired more and more Black teachers during the first part of the 1970s.

TABLE 3-17* **POPULATION OF TEACHERS AND STUDENTS BY YEAR AND RACE**				
YEAR	**TEACHERS**		**STUDENTS**	
	BLACK	**WHITE**	**BLACK**	**WHITE**
1970	407	2,904	28,176	39,318
7971	445	2,908	28,040	39,547
1972	516	2,829	28,706	40,961
1973	547	2,712	28,218	39,237
*"Report of Staff Racial Census," Pittsburgh Board of Education, 1974, pages 1-4.				

The data show that the Black teacher population increased from 1970 to 1973 (the final year of the study), while the White teacher population decreased. The author asked the personnel department at the Board of Education to explain this phenomenon. The following explanations were offered.

Under the pressure of civil rights groups, teachers, and the ever-increasing ratio of Black students, the Board hired Blacks to replace White teachers who left or retired. It was also indicated that proportionately more Black teachers were presenting themselves to the Board as potential teachers. Still another explanation offered was that many Whites were applying for positions outside the Pittsburgh school system because they would rather not have to teach in inner-city schools. It seems likely that all of these reasons may offer some explanation for the phenomenon. As the preceding show, the number of White teachers decreased from 1970 to 1973, but the number of White students remained fairly stable. It is obvious then that the White teachers were not following a population shift relative to White students. It is equally obvious that they could not have been fleeing a rapidly growing Black student population because that number also remained fairly constant.

Conversations with the author about the treatment of these Black teachers hired in the 1970s revealed that almost all of those interviewed felt that a great deal of racism was exhibited by their White counterparts toward Black students. They felt that most of the White teachers did not understand, did not respect, and did not like Black students. They felt that many of the White teachers did not make any sincere effort to teach Black youngsters who did not "behave like White ladies and gentlemen." The Black teachers also felt that many of the White teachers would not teach in inner-city schools if they could find jobs elsewhere. Several young White teachers who spoke with the author shared this view.

The Black teachers hired in the 1970s said that, while the White teachers were cordial to them, they (the Blacks) felt tolerated by their counterparts. They also expressed the same sort of reservations about the officials at the Pittsburgh Board of Education as well as the top administrative staff of the Board. They felt, however, that they got along fairly well with White parents. Relationships between them and students, both Black and White, were classified as very good.

While it is entirely possible that racist behavior on the part of White teachers may have increased in the later years of the study, it is unlikely that this is the only reason for the complaints by Black teachers. It is likely that another contributing factor is the increased awareness of young Black teachers and their unwillingness to accept treatment and behavior which might have gone unchallenged in prior years."

Since Lawrence Peeler was hired in 1937, the progress of Black teachers in the Pittsburgh Public School system has been steady and impressive. Complete data for all years were unavailable since, for many years, Blacks were listed in the Board of Education statistics only as "professional" and non-professional. What can be said with certainty is that the number of Black teachers employed in the Pittsburgh Public School system increased from one in 1937 to 547 by 1973, the last year of the study.

Summary and Conclusions

In 1937, the first Black full-time school teacher was hired by the Pittsburgh Board of Public Education since the days of the "colored schools" which had been closed before the turn of the century. From evidence examined it is obvious that it would have taken at least several more years for the Board of Education to hire Black teachers had it not been for the 1937 Pennsylvania Legislative Hearings into the discriminatory hiring practices of the Pittsburgh Board of Education.

This first hiring in the twentieth century did not result in more Black teachers being hired immediately. It appears that the Board simply sat back as if it had fulfilled its obligation by that one single act. It also appears that Blacks themselves did not press the advantage they had gained as a result of the Legislative Hearings. There is no evidence to suggest that Blacks continued to put pressure on the members of the Board of Education to hire more than a token Black teacher. Perhaps if Blacks had continued their pressure, the hiring of Blacks would have proceeded at a more rapid pace.

The next nine Blacks employed by the School Board (this too until 1943) included a music teacher, an activities director, a truant officer, and six physical education teachers. All but two were employed in elementary schools located in the Hill District—Pittsburgh's largest Black ghetto.

As more Blacks became aware that there was a possibility of employment with the Public School system, they applied in increasing numbers. Some even returned from other states to seek positions in the Pittsburgh Public Schools.

At this stage, the Pittsburgh Board of Education began to practice another form of discrimination, that of systematically placing Black teachers in elementary schools located in the Hill District. Under increasing pressure from Black teachers themselves, the Board resumed hiring Black teachers in 1945; again, these teachers were confined to schools located in the Hill District.

The discrimination pattern changed in 1950 when, for the first time, Blacks were hired for teaching positions outside the Hill. All four of those Blacks were assigned to elementary schools. For whatever reasons, it is apparent that the Board had decided that Blacks had to prove themselves on the elementary level before they would be allowed to teach in the secondary schools. Later, Blacks would be hired to teach in secondary schools outside of the Black community; however, this did not take place until the mid-1950s.

From the 1950s on, progress made by Black teachers was much more dramatic partly because of increased internal pressure from Black teachers and partly because of the external pressure caused by the civil rights movement of the 1960s and 1970s. It is also apparent that the composition of the Board of Education itself was changing as overt racists were replaced by more liberal members and by a small number of Blacks.

Another trend occurred during this time. As the number of Black teachers increased, the number of White teachers declined.

It is obvious that the Pittsburgh Board of Education hired teachers on a discriminatory basis for most of the years from 1937 to 1973 and that the nature and scope of that discrimination changed over time. Despite these practices, Blacks made steady and significant progress.

**Protest in Front of Pittsburgh Board of
Education Administration Offices – c. 1968**

Children Protesting loss of local school

CHAPTER 4

Internal Pressure: More Blacks in Professional Positions

In the previous chapter the numerical increase in the number of Black teachers in the Pittsburgh Public School system was examined. Once in the system, these teachers exerted increasing pressure on the Board of Education. This pressure resulted in a variety of changes including the hiring of Black administrators, principals and counselors, changes in textbooks, the treatment of Black students, and Black involvement in extracurricular activities.

Guidance Counselors

Even though Blacks had begun to make progress as teachers, the area of guidance counseling remained the exclusive domain of White teachers. Counselors in the Pittsburgh Public School system had traditionally been chosen from the ranks of teachers, yet from 1937 to 1960 no Blacks were appointed as counselors.

Counseling had been a point of friction between the Board of Education and the Black community for many years, because Blacks felt that white counselors were not giving sound advice to Black youngsters. It was also evident by their treatment of Black youngsters that the White counselors cared little about the fate of Black students. Often, when summer jobs were available for students, these jobs were dispensed through the counselors. More often than not, Black students never heard about the jobs until they had been filled by White students.

Many felt that it was impossible for White middle-class counselors to advise or counsel Black youngsters, because the counselors knew little or nothing about the background from which the Black youngsters came. These counselors did not recognize the validity of Black culture and insisted upon treating Black youngsters as some aberrant form of White children.

Often, Black teachers took it upon themselves to provide Black students with the counseling that they were not getting from those Whites who were acting in counseling roles. Alice Bernice Wade reports that she and Bob Munjin decided that Black students at Fifth Avenue High School were not being given adequate counseling and assistance by the White counselors when it came time to enter college, so she and Munjin wrote to colleges on behalf of the Blacks and succeeded in getting some of them into college. This role was very clearly the responsibility of the White counselor.

Mrs. Wade also told of going to the Board of Education to be interviewed for a counseling position. She said she was turned down because they stated that she showed too much favoritism toward Blacks. Mrs. Wade claims that later the Board hired a White woman to fill the position, who was far less qualified. Mary Louise Stone, who was also concerned about the lack of adequate counseling for Blacks, formed a college club at Fifth Avenue to help Black youngsters get into college.[1]

The author quite vividly recalls going through thirteen years of school in the Pittsburgh system and never seeing a Black counselor. He recalls being advised to take shop courses and go to a trade school rather than take academic courses or to think about college. White students were referred to summer jobs; Blacks were not. White students got scholarships to colleges and assistance in filling out applications; Blacks (for the most part) did not. In fact, the only scholarships the author got were those he had arranged to get through his own efforts. It soon became clear to most Blacks that the White counselors were not interested in them, so they avoided the counselor's office at all times. One other memory remains vivid about White counselors—they always seemed very surprised when Black students did well on standardized IQ or achievement tests.

---

1   Alice Bernice Wade and Mary Louise Stone, in discussion with the author, 1975.

Finally, the long, dry spell was over when, in February 1960, Helen Faison became the city's first Black counselor.[2] She was assigned to Westinghouse High School at a time when the school was already predominantly Black, as it had been since 1955, yet no Black counselor had been assigned to the school for five years after it became a "Black" school. At the time of Mrs. Faison's appointment, the school population included 1,897 Black students and 344 Whites.[3] Shortly after Mrs. Faison's appointment, William Green was also assigned to Westinghouse as the second Black counselor in the city.[4]

Among the other Blacks hired as counselors during the 1960s was Christine Fulwylie in 1963 at Oliver High School. At the time of her appointment, the Black student population at Oliver was 418, while the White student enrollment was 885. In 1966, Paul Williams was appointed as a counselor at Herron Hill Jr. High School, which had one White student out of an enrollment of 1002 students. In 1968, Ollie Mae Guice became the second Black counselor at Peabody High School, having been preceded by Ed Ray. Peabody had been an integrated school for some time. In 1968, the student population was 461 Blacks, 2126 Whites.[5]

For the most part, Blacks who became counselors related that they were treated pretty well by White administrators, faculty and staff, as well as by students. Most also indicated that they received an enthusiastic reception from Black students and parents.[6]

Herman McClain relates the following about his experiences as a counselor. McClain returned to the Pittsburgh Public School system after a three-year absence. In 1972, he was asked to take an assignment as a counselor at John Morrow Elementary School on the upper North Side, and McClain became the first Black male teacher in the school. The school had a small Black student population, most of whom were bussed in from the lower North Side. McClain indicated that his presence seemed to polarize the entire staff. Some were his staunch supporters; others had little to do with him. He also felt that the school

2   Pittsburgh Board of Education, Personnel Office, 1976.
3   Pittsburgh Board of Education, Statistics Office.
4   Frank Bolden, (Pittsburgh Board of Education, Office for Public Information) in discussion with the author, 1976.
5   Pittsburgh Board of Education, Statistics Office.
6   Black Counselors in discussion with the author, 1973.

administration had done little to sensitize the White faculty to the needs of the Black students who were being bussed in. The teachers didn't get to know the Black students and knew nothing of the area from which the students came. McClain felt the teachers needed more counseling than the students, so he tried to set up counseling sessions for staff. He is sure that these counseling sessions are what led to his transfer later in 1972. When McClain went to Langley as a counselor in that year, the West End school was still predominantly White. He feels he was treated well by the faculty, contrasting markedly with his treatment at John Morrow.[7]

Blacks continued to make progress as counselors, although that progress was not as dramatic as the progress Black teachers had made. By 1970, there were 20 Black counselors and 68 White counselors. There were 2,904 White teachers and 407 Black teachers.[8] While the simple numerical increase in the number of Black counselors may not be as impressive as those for teachers, in actuality there was a larger percentage of Black counselors than Black teachers (12.3% of the teachers were Black, while 22.8% of the counselors were Black). By 1973, the last year of this study, Blacks comprised approximately 27.8 % of the counseling staff (28 of 101), and approximately 16.8% of the teacher population (547 of 3,259).[9]

Principals

Black teachers began to exert pressure on the Board of Education for appointments as principals and vice-principals. For many years this pressure was ignored. Even schools with a nearly total Black population had White principals and vice-principals. It is impossible to accurately reconstruct data on principals and vice-principals, because of insufficient statistics at the Board of Education. However, it can be stated that from 1937 until 1955 there were no Black principals or vice-principals in the Pittsburgh Public School system. In 1955, John Brewer, who had been one of the first Black teachers in Pittsburgh

---

7 Herman McClain in discussion with the author, 1976.
8 *Staff Racial Census Report*, Pittsburgh Board of Education, 1971.
9 *Staff Racial Census Report*, Pittsburgh Board of Education, 1974.

during the 20th century, was appointed the first Black principal in the history of the Pittsburgh Public School system.[10]

Brewer was assigned to Miller Elementary School, which is located in the Hill and was, at the time of his appointment, almost totally Black. There were only 17 White students in a population of 912 students.[11] The only other Black to be appointed to an administrative role in the 1950s was Jody Harris, who was made vice-principal of Herron Hill Jr. High in 1959.[12] At the time of Mr. Harris' appointment, Herron Hill had 773 Black students and nine Whites.[13] Once again, discrimination changed, yet remained the same: the Board finally hired a Black principal, but he was assigned to a Black elementary school in a Black neighborhood. Always, up to this date, the first moves, the first faltering steps, were taken at the elementary school level. The second Black was also placed in a predominantly Black school in the Black community.

Blacks continued to make progress during the 1960s in securing positions as principals and vice-principals. Some were to become principals in predominantly Black schools; others would become principals in schools with a more racially balanced student population. One person, Emma Florine Robinson, established an impressive list of firsts, both during the 1960s and the 1970s. She was the first Black principal at Philip Murray Elementary School in Mount Oliver, Larimer Elementary School in East Liberty, and Arsenal Elementary School in the Arsenal District.[14]

It was thought by many Blacks that, when the White principal of Herron Hill Jr. High School resigned, his logical successor would be Jody Harris, who had established a fine reputation first as a teacher at Herron Hill and Schenley High School, and then as vice-principal at Herron Hill. In 1964, Harris was passed over in favor of a White man in his quest to become the first Black principal in the history of Herron Hill Jr. High. A *Pittsburgh Courier* article that year reported that a group of Black and White citizens had picketed the Board over its failure to promote Mr. Harris. The same article said that Mr. Harris

10 Frank Bolden, 1976.
11 Pittsburgh Board of Education, Statistics Office.
12 Frank Bolden, 1976.
13 Pittsburgh Board of Education, Statistics Office.
14 Frank Bolden, 1976.

was to be promoted to a position as Supervisor of Vocational Education at the Board.[15]

Alice Bernice Wade, who was a teacher in the system at this time, was one of the people who picketed the Board over this refusal to promote Jody Harris. She talked with the author about this incident. "They did Jody wrong. He was already the vice-principal, but they wouldn't elevate Jody. Instead, they took some White elementary school teacher and put him in as principal. I picketed the Board with some other people; my supervisor came out of the building and said I would be fired if I didn't stop picketing."[16]

Mr. Harris was so disheartened by the treatment he had received from the administration that he resigned and left the city in 1966. Prior to his resignation, Harris was appointed as an assistant principal at South Hills High School. It would have been the first time a Black person had served as an assistant principal in a predominantly White school. Harris said, "In all my years of teaching I have never seen a Black appointed to the principalship of a Pittsburgh high school... The Board of Education has not done all it could do in the matter of upgrading its own veteran Blacks."[17]

After many years of pressure and bad feelings from the Black community, the Pittsburgh Board of Education finally appointed the first Black principal to Herron Hill Jr. High School. Elmo Calloway was named to that post in 1967. Most Black residents could not believe that the process had taken so much time, especially since Herron Hill had been a predominantly Black school since 1933. At the time of Mr. Calloway's appointment, there was one White student among the 921 students attending Herron Hill. Mr. Calloway had become the first Black vice-principal at Conroy School on the North Side in 1963. At the time, Conroy, too, was a predominantly Black school, with 490 Black students and 209 White students.[18]

In 1962, Gertrude Wade became the first Black principal in the long history of Robert L. Vann School in the Hill District, one of the city's largest Black ghettos. She also was the first Black female

---

15 *The Pittsburgh Courier*, September 5, 1964, page 1.
16 Alice Bernice Wade in discussion with the author, 1973.
17 *The Pittsburgh Courier*, August 6, 1966, page 1.
18 Statistics in this paragraph and the next six paragraphs are from Pittsburgh Board of Education, Statistics Office.

principal in the city. Vann, like the other schools in the area, had been predominantly Black since the 1930s, but it took the Board until 1962 to name a Black principal. In 1962, Vann had but two White students in a total enrollment of 823 students. Later, in 1967, Mrs. Wade became the first Black principal at Larimer Elementary School in East Liberty. This school, too, was, in keeping with the prevalent practice of assigning Black principals to Black schools. It was nearly totally Black, having 554 Black students and 84 Whites.

By 1968, Perry High School on the North Side was still predominantly White. There were only 190 Black students in a total student population of 1,508. The Board deviated from its usual practice by assigning a Black principal that year, Mr. John Young.

Manchester is a district in the lower North Side; its population had been predominantly Black for quite some time. In fact, Manchester was one of the largest Black ghettos in Pittsburgh. Manchester Elementary School had been a predominantly Black school since 1955. By 1968, the Black student population was 695 and the White student population was 76. The Board did not appoint its first Black principal for Manchester Elementary until 1968, when Ted Vassar was appointed. Mr. Vassar had been principal of Fort Pitt Elementary in 1967. Later, in 1970, he would become principal of Westinghouse High.[19]

Homewood had also been a mixed neighborhood for many years. In the mid-1950s, it became a predominantly Black neighborhood. In 1955, Westinghouse High School went the way of the neighborhood, yet the Board refrained from appointing the first Black principal until 1968. In that year, Paul Williams became the school's first Black principal. The population of the school when Williams took over contained only 21 White students in a total population of 2,829.

In 1968, Helen Faison became the first Black principal ever appointed to a Pittsburgh high school. This includes all the years the public schools had operated in both the nineteenth and twentieth centuries. Fifth Avenue High School, like most other schools in the Hill, had been an all-Black school for decades. By the time Mrs. Faison took over the reins as principal, there were 1,233 Black students and 43 White students. Mrs. Faison had previously been a vice-principal at Westinghouse High School in 1963.

---

19 Ted Vassar in dicusssion with the author, 1975.

Another Black to become the first principal of her race in a particular school was Myrna Sumpter, who was appointed to Belmar Elementary School in Homewood in 1966. The school then contained 996 Black students and 6 White students. This was another example of the Board's not hiring a Black principal until the school was nearly all Black.

Other Blacks who were appointed to principal positions during the 1960s were:

Doris G. Brevard, Robert L. Vann Elementary School, District, 1969. The school was predominantly Black;

Audia Mae Gilliard, Vice-principal, Westinghouse High School, Homewood, 1969—a predominantly Black school;

John Lewis, Vice-principal, Oliver High School, North Side, 1967—a predominantly White school, but only by 220 students;

Lois Golden, Vice-principal, Schenley High School, Oakland, 1969—a 100 % Black school;

Christine Fulwylie, Vice-principal, Fifth Avenue High School, 1965—a predominantly Black school;

Robert Cook, Vice-principal, Fifth Avenue High School, 1968—a predominantly Black school.[20]

Did this group of Blacks, who were among the first to be hired as principals and vice-principals, experience the same kinds of problems the first Black teachers experienced? The author asked this question in a series of interviews conducted with the previously mentioned individuals.[21] Almost all of them reported experiencing no major difficulties. Some indicated that they had sensed some animosity or insecurity from parents. Myrna Sumpter said that it was difficult for some of the parents to deal with a Black woman as the principal of

---

20 Frank Bolden, 1976.
21 Black Principals in discussion with the author, 1973-1977.

her school. Paul Williams said he had one run-in with a parent, but on the whole all those interviewed felt they had been treated well as principals. Perhaps one reason for this apparently good treatment was that one gets less static and harassment as a principal than one does as a teacher. While all those the author spoke to pretty much agreed that they were treated well as principals and vice-principals, they also nearly all agreed that they were certain that their progress through the system would have been faster had they been White.

In 1970, Myrna Sumpter was assigned as the first Black principal of Linden Elementary School in the eastern part of the city. This marked the first time a Black principal had been assigned to a predominantly White elementary school. Up to that point, the Board had been subjecting the Black principals to the same practice used on Black teachers previously – assigning Blacks to predominantly Black schools and only much later assigning them to predominantly White schools. Linden then had only 44 Black students and 611 White students.[22] In an interview with the author, Mrs. Sumpter indicated that she was treated as well as can be expected under the circumstances. She said many people came into her office to "get a look at this new principal." She was also aware of some negative feelings in the community about her being appointed to the post, but none of those feelings surfaced in any sort of conflict."[23]

Sunnyside Elementary School, in the Arsenal section of the city, got its first Black principal in 1971 in the person of Willa White. Though integrated, Sunnyside had only 12 Black students. The White population numbered 585 students.[24] In spite of the fact that there were only two Black teachers at the school, Mrs. White feels she was well treated. She felt she had an advantage over some other people who might have been assigned there, because she had attended Sunnyside with many of the parents of the children who were now attending the school. Most problems, therefore, could be resolved with a quick telephone call.[25]

Ernest Huddle was appointed to Langley High School as its first Black vice-principal in 1970. Langley is located in the Sheridan District on the South Side of Pittsburgh. At the time of Mr. Huddle's

---

22 Pittsburgh Board of Education, Statistics Office.
23 Myrna Sumpter in discussion with the author, 1975.
24 Pittsburgh Board of Education, Statistics Office.
25 Willa White in discussion with the author, 1973.

appointment, the school was "slightly" integrated, having a Black student population of 313 in a total student population of 2,197.[26] Mr. Huddle said he had no major problems with faculty, staff, students or parents. He does recall a couple of racially inspired incidents, however. In one instance, a White parent called Mr. Huddle and accused him of suspending only White students. In another, a parent called and asked him, "What are you doing about the coons up there?" Huddle said he replied, "Oh, I didn't know we had any." Later, the man's son mentioned that Mr. Huddle was Black; Huddle said the man did not even have the courage to call him and apologize. Instead, the man called the White vice-principal and apologized to Mr. Huddle through the White man.[27]

Robert Cook, who had tried to enter the system as a teacher in 1946, but who was unable to get a job with the Board until 1952, was made a principal in 1970. He was appointed to Conroy School on the North Side. Conroy was, by then, a "Black" school with 279 Black students and 25 Whites.[28] Mr. Cook felt that members of his faculty did exhibit some racist tendencies both toward him and Black students.

Irv Biggs was appointed assistant principal of Frick School in Oakland in 1970. While not the first Black assistant principal at the school, Mr. Biggs was among the first few. By 1970, Frick, too, was a predominantly Black school. Of 1,008 students, 876 were Black. Mr. Biggs told the author that "the school was all mucked up. It had had a succession of White Ph.D.'s (as principals) who were not concerned with the rapid change in the population." Biggs indicated that the main problem was teacher turnover. He attributed this to the unwillingness of many White teachers to teach in a predominantly Black school. Biggs related that his own daughter had gone to the school and had seven math teachers in six months. After staying at Frick for less than a year, Biggs was assigned to Northview Heights Elementary School. Even though the school had been integrated since 1963, and had been predominantly Black since 1969, Biggs, in 1970, was the first Black principal. In 1970, there were 1,134 Black students and 36 Whites. That constituted an extremely rapid change because in 1963, when the school

---

26 Pittsburgh Board Education, Office of Statistics.
27 Ernest Huddle in discussion with the author, 1975.
28 Statistics in this paragraph and the next are from the Pittsburgh Board of Education, Statistics Office.

opened, there were 282 Blacks and 572 Whites. At Northview, Biggs faced the same problems he faced at Frick—a rapidly shifting racial composition in the student body and a high rate of teacher turnover. Again, Biggs encountered a great many racist teachers on the faculty. He indicated that when he came to Northview about 75 % of the White teachers wanted to transfer because the school was "too bad." Biggs said that what they actually meant was that there were too many Black kids going to the school. Biggs felt that one kind of pervasive racism one had to face is teachers who either could not or would not deal with culturally different children.[29]

Blacks made significant progress in the positions of principal and vice-principal during the years of this study, rising from zero percent in 1937-1954 to 35% by 1973 (59 of 169). Table 4-1 shows the growth of the Black population of principals/vice-principals since 1937. Interestingly, in 1973 Black teachers formed less than 17% of the total teacher population in the Pittsburgh Public Schools (547 of 3259). Black principals formed 35% of the total principal population. The author could find no one who could explain this situation. Perhaps more Blacks were pushing to become principals because of the added prestige, money, and authority that go along with those positions.

---

29 Irv Briggs in discussion with the author, 1975.

TABLE 4-1* INCREASE IN NUMBER OF BLACK PRINCIPALS & VICE-PRINCIPALS BY YEAR	
YEAR(S)	NUMBER
1937 - 1954	0
1955 – 1958	1
1959 – 1961	2
1962	3
1963	9
1964	19
1965 – 1967	No data
1968	29
1969	33
1970	48
1971	53
1972	56
1973	59
*Compiled from racial census reports obtained from Pittsburgh Board of Education	

Board of Education Central Staff

Since Blacks were being hired as teachers, counselors and principals and vice-principals, it might be expected that the Board of Public Education would have been moving, by the 1950s, toward placing Black professionals on the central staff and employing them in the administrative offices in the Oakland section. Unfortunately for Blacks, such was not the case. As more Blacks moved into positions of principals, vice-principals, and counselors in the schools, they began to look for places to move that would provide them with upward mobility; the logical place was the Board's central administrative offices. As a result of internal pressure from these professionals and external pressures from the Black community, the Board of Education hired its first Black central staff member in 1961. In that year Robert Woodruff was appointed Assistant Director of Team Teaching.[30]

---

30 Frank Bolden, 1976.

In 1964, the second Black central staff member was hired. He was Frank Bolden, who was made Assistant Director of Information Services and Community Relations. In the same year, John Brewer was appointed Assistant Director of School and Community Affairs.[31]

While this might be considered progress by some, most Black leaders considered it mere tokenism.[32] The Education Department of the Urban League of Pittsburgh expressed its views about teacher integration in Pittsburgh in this way:

> . . . Yet we are troubled by the fact that we know of no Negro principal, vice-principal or assistant principals who are not in a school with a predominantly Negro enrollment, that the highest-ranking educational officer is an assistant director of the Compensatory Education Program and that all of the appointments at or above the level of Assistant Superintendent before and since 1963 have been white. [33]

Due to the unavailability of accurate records, it is impossible to chart the progress of Black professionals on the central staff of the Board of Education. From available data it can be determined that by 1970 the following people had been placed on the central administrative staff:

---

31 Frank Bolden, 1976.

32 Black Leaders in discussion with the author, 1973-1977.

33 Untitled Urban League of Pittsburgh document dated October 10, 1965, found in the files of the Pittsburgh NAACP, located in the Archives of the Industrial Society, University of Pittsburgh, Hillman Library.

TABLE 4-2 BLACK PROFESSIONALS ON BOARD ADMINISTRATIVE STAFF, 1970	
Herb Parrish	Deputy Superintendent
Helen Faison	Deputy Superintendent
Elmo Calloway	Deputy Superintendent
Sarah Harvey	Deputy Superintendent
Paul Williams	Deputy Superintendent
Lawrence Peeler	School Reorganization
William Green	Pupil Service Department
Robert Woodruff	Pupil Service Department
Christine Fulwylie	Pupil Service Department

Since the data available made it impossible to isolate each professional category for the years of this study, I have attempted to chart the progress of Black professionals as a whole for the years of the study. Table 4-3 charts the progress of Black professionals from 1937 to 1973, both by number and percentage.

TABLE 4-3 INCREASE IN BLACK PROFESSIONALS BY NUMBER, YEAR, AND % OF ALL PROFESSIONAL STAFF*		
YEAR	**NUMBER**	**%**
1937	1	.0003
1938	2	.0003
1939	3	.0003
1940	3	.0003
1941	4	.0003
1942	9	.0004
1943	Data Not Available	
1944		
1945	25	.9
1946	27	1.1
1947	30	1.9

1948	40	2.0
1949	50	2.1
1950	52	2.2
1951	Data Not Available	
1952	60	3.0
1953	75	3.5
1954	105	4.1
1955	137	5.3
1956	156	5.9
1957	179	6.8
1958	205	7.7
1959	218	8.1
1960	226	8.4
1961	243	8.7
1962	270	9.1
1963	287	9.4
1964	301	9.8
1965	310	10.0
1966	350	10.1
1967	402	11.1
1968	440	12.3
1969	459	13.1
1970	480	13.5
1971	527	14.6
1972	611	16.7
1973	644	18.0

*Data from 1937-1944 obtained from interviews, newspaper accounts, and other sources.
Data from 1945-1970 compiled from *Racial Census of Staff* reports, Pittsburgh Board of Education.
Data for 1971-1973 compiled from racial census reports, Pittsburgh Board of Education.

Other Pressures, Other Changes

While it is relatively simple to reconstruct the progress Blacks made in employment as teachers and the pressure they exerted for other professional positions, it is more difficult to discern what other effects resulted from the pressure exerted by Black teachers on the School Board and the school system in general. From the interviews conducted for this paper, the author discovered some other areas in which changes came about as a result of this internal pressure.

One of these areas was in the self-concept of Black students. Several of the Black teachers indicated that they had run-ins with White teachers who were attempting to make Black students feel stupid. The Black teachers helped the students to realize that they were not stupid and that they could learn. Many of the Black teachers spoke of holding extra tutoring sessions with Black students to make up for the White teachers who refused to teach Black youngsters.[34]

The presence of Black teachers also exerted pressure on White teachers and administrators to treat Black students better than they had been treated in the past. Many of the overt racist practices and remarks abated in the presence of Black teachers. Several Black teachers remarked that they felt that the very fact that Black teachers were present made many White teachers more aware of their own prejudices.

Pressure was also put on Black students to do better in school. The Black teachers provided important role models for Black students. The author recalls the particular pride he felt when these Black teachers took an interest in him and how badly he felt when he thought he had disappointed them. In addition, these Black role models made it difficult for racist teachers to perpetuate the myth of the lack of Black accomplishment.

As has been mentioned previously, Black teachers also changed, to some extent, the counseling practices of Whites. In some cases, Black teachers counseled Black youngsters on their own time since it was obvious that White counselors were not providing Black youngsters with proper counseling. This forced some White counselors to begin to provide Black students with information about jobs and colleges since

---

34 Black teachers in discussion with the author, 1973 - 1976.

it was likely that the Black students would receive this information from Black teachers.[35]

Still another area of influence was curriculum development and teaching materials. Some of the teachers interviewed spoke of pressuring the Board of Education to introduce Black history into the classroom. Others spoke of introducing their own teaching materials having to do with the Black experience rather than relying on the irrelevant materials provided by the Board of Education. Black teachers forced the removal of such books as *Little Black Sambo* from the classrooms and libraries. Black teachers applied increasing pressure on the Board of Education to introduce books and teaching materials which had some relationship to the Black experience.[36]

Black students had traditionally been excluded from significant participation in extra-curricular activities. This exclusion extended to plays, debate clubs, school newspapers, as well as a variety of other activities. While doing the research for this paper, the author found many instances related by both former students and teachers in which Blacks had been purposely excluded from extra-curricular activities by both the staff and administration of the Public School system.

As more Blacks were hired in teaching and counseling roles, this situation slowly changed. Many of the teachers interviewed spoke of becoming involved in the directing and sponsoring of extra-curricular activities so that they could be certain their Black students were being given ample opportunities to become involved. Some sponsored debate clubs. Still others held informal rap sessions and groups designed to increase the self-esteem of Black students. Some teachers made their contribution by encouraging Black students to become involved in extra-curricular activities while they (the Black teachers) monitored the treatment Black students received from Whites who directed the activities. The Black teachers felt that Black students were treated more fairly when the White activity director knew that Black teachers were watching them closely.

Black teachers exerted pressure on the varsity sports program. Black students had always been discriminated against in sports, even

---

35 Black Counselors in discussion with the author, 1973 - 1976.
36 Black teachers in discussion with the author, 1973 - 1976.

though most people believe discrimination does not exist in the sports arena. Many students and teachers complained about how their teams may have been better if Black athletes had been properly utilized. It was difficult, at times, to discern that discrimination was taking place because of the nature of the athletic teams. It was difficult for a coach to discriminate in some sports, such as track and field, where participation is based on easily demonstrated qualities such as the ability to run faster, jump higher, put a shot or throw a discus further than anyone else.

It was easier to discriminate in soccer, basketball or football simply by positions assigned or combination of players used. If, for instance, a basketball player is assigned the position of defensive forward rather than one of the other positions, he is less likely to become a high scorer on the team. By the same token, if Blacks are made defensive backs in football, their chances of becoming stars are greatly diminished. Another form of sports discrimination was "stacking"—i.e., putting most of the Blacks in the same position so that they compete with one another for that position rather than having the opportunity to compete with Whites for more prestigious positions, such as quarterback. Another type of discrimination took the form of simply using Black players far less frequently than Whites.

The author recalls that throughout all his years of competitive sports, starting in the seventh grade, there was not one Black coach in either Herron Hill or Schenley High. (The author graduated from Schenley in 1956.) During that time, Blacks were discriminated against in football, soccer, basketball, and baseball. When the author played football at Schenley High, one backfield was composed of all Blacks. This backfield was clearly the best combination of offensive players on the entire team. Yet these Black players were never used in combination, but were always broken up in such a manner as to make certain that there were no more than two Blacks in the backfield at any one time. We were forced to play with a White quarterback far less skilled than the Black quarterback. Black football players at Schenley were also discriminated against by the practice of picking first string players from those students whose parents were able to afford to pay the fee for attending football camp in the summer. If one did not attend the camp, he did not make the team, except as a substitute.

As Black teachers moved into coaching, the discriminatory practices decreased and Blacks were allowed to pursue sports on a more equal basis. Black coaches allowed Black students to "be themselves." The author recalls the state champion Schenley High basketball team being allowed to wear a floppy type of hat on the court during warm-ups and being allowed to clown around and enjoy their warm-up sessions before games. The Black coach encouraged this, saying it relaxed the players; it was the way they behaved during practice, and it allowed them to play their own type of game. In previous years, under White coaching, these antics would have been labeled undignified and the students would have been forced to be chocolate carbon copies of White players.

Summary and Conclusions

Once Black teachers had been hired in significant numbers in the Pittsburgh Public School system, they began to exert internal pressure on that system. This pressure resulted in Blacks being appointed to previously all-White positions such as vice-principal, principal, counselor and administrative positions on the central staff of the Board of Education. It is likely that Black progress in these positions would have been much slower had it not been for this internal pressure. It is apparent that there was not much external pressure on the Board to appoint Blacks to any positions other than teaching. The NAACP, the Urban League, and other Black organizations were not involved in an organized effort in these areas. It was up to the Black teachers themselves to make their own paths, and this they did without much fanfare or glory or much notice. They, by their persistent pressure on their supervisors and other administrators, opened the doors for Blacks to positions previously held only by Whites.

It is also likely that, in some cases, this pressure was viewed favorably by the people who were being pressured. It is evident that some White administrators were more liberal than their predecessors and did not attempt to actively block the advancement of Blacks into nontraditional positions. However, it must be stated that most of the Blacks interviewed felt that the sympathetic White administrator was the exception rather than the rule.

The Black teachers, having secured employment as teachers, were not content to simply teach. They turned their attention to the problems of unfair treatment of Black students by White staff and administrators. Their efforts resulted in Black students being treated more fairly in varsity sports and in other extra-curricular activities. White teachers tended to treat Black students with more respect, especially when monitored by Black teachers. When Blacks were appointed vice-principals or principals it is likely that White teachers were even more careful about their treatment of Black students.

One cannot say for certain that changes in the treatment of the Black student population would not have changed over time. It is likely that at the height of the civil rights movement of the 1960s, those dramatic changes would have taken place. The fact is that these changes were already underway thanks to the pressure of the Black teachers.

One theme kept repeating throughout this entire study—i.e., in almost every instance, when Blacks made progress in the public education system, there was a "trade-off." By that I mean that when one examines the patterns of discrimination in the Pittsburgh educational system, Blacks made progress in one area only to find later that they had traded one form of discrimination for another. When Blacks won the right to free public education for their children, the trade-off was that school was held in the basements of Black churches. When they won the right to an education in a school building, the trade-off was a segregated "colored school" with a primarily White teaching staff. Blacks pushed for integration and traded the "colored" system for an integrated system which employed no full-time Black teachers for a number of years.

When Black teachers became employed in the late 1930s and early 1940s, the trade-off was confinement to predominantly Black elementary schools in Black communities. They were also restricted initially to certain subject areas. When Blacks pushed to be accepted in subject areas other than physical education and music, the trade-off was being allowed to teach only in Black elementary schools.

The trade-off principle is evident again when Blacks won teaching assignments outside of the Black ghettos but were confined to elementary schools. Blacks won appointments as counselors, but had to do their counseling in Black schools. Black teachers won appointments in secondary schools, but only in ghetto schools. Black vice-principals seemed to take an unduly long time in rising to the position of principal and, again, they had to "prove" themselves in Black elementary schools in Black communities.

Later, Blacks gained positions on the administrative staff of the Board of Education's central office. The trade-off was that generally the jobs were not commensurate with their skills and training. Few held any hopes of ever becoming a Supervisor in the school system.

Again and again Blacks made progress in one area only to find that there was yet another area of discrimination to be tackled. Many of these early teachers were pioneers, in their own sense charting new paths for other Blacks to follow and steadily chipping away at the wall of prejudice and discrimination erected by the Pittsburgh Board of Public Education. The wall is not down yet, but thanks to people like James Peeler, John Brewer and others, this wall is beginning to crumble.

Girls Drill Team in School Yard

**Students from Homewood School
on field trip to Allegheny Observatory**

Students learning how to operate press in machine shop

Students displaying lamp stands in woodworking shop

Students and teacher in Music Class

Westinghouse High School Orchestra Rehearsal

Children eating lunch in school cafeteria

CHAPTER 5

Concluding Summary

The discrimination faced by Black teachers in Pittsburgh was not a simple issue. The pattern of discrimination changed and shifted, ebbed and flowed, and changed in scope and intensity over the entire time span of the study. When Pittsburgh began free public education in 1834, Black children were excluded from attendance at the public schools. The education of Black youngsters was a hit-and-miss proposition until 1837, when the Board of Education gave in to pressure from Black citizens and opened a "colored school." For the years that this separate system existed, a few Black teachers were hired to teach the Black students, but most of the teachers were White.

In 1881, the separate Black school system came to an end. Unfortunately, so did the employment of Black teachers. Apparently the Central Board of Education felt that it was not acceptable for Black teachers to teach White pupils. At any rate, from 1881 until 1933, no Blacks were hired to teach even on a part-time basis in the Pittsburgh Public Schools and it was not until 1937 that the first fulltime Black teacher was hired.

Blacks brought pressure on the Board of Education to hire Black teachers, but prior to 1937, their efforts were in vain as the Board of Education used a variety of techniques to deny employment to Blacks. Despite Black protest, the Pittsburgh Public School System lagged behind other Northern and Southern cities in the hiring of Black teachers. The resistance on the part of the Pittsburgh Board of Public Education can be attributed to a number of factors, which were detailed in this study.

The hiring of the first Black teacher in twentieth century Pittsburgh did not mean an end to discriminatory practices. The Board of Education simply substituted other forms of discrimination. First, they moved very slowly in hiring other Blacks; by 1943 there were but nine Black professionals in the Pittsburgh public school system. Second, they relegated Blacks to assignments in predominantly Black elementary schools in one Black community, The Hill District. Although the Hill District was only one of several neighborhoods with large Black populations, it was not until 1950 that Blacks received their first teaching assignments outside of the Hill. Third, the Blacks hired to teach outside of the Hill were confined to elementary schools. Fourth, even after they were hired, these early Black teachers were restricted to certain subject areas which had been deemed suitable for Black teachers.

What appears to have developed was a trade-off system. It is not certain that Blacks were always aware of the operation of this system but it was very much in evidence. When a gain was made in one area related to education the tradeoff was the acceptance, if only temporarily, of another form of discrimination. For example, when Blacks gained an integrated educational system for their children the tradeoff was the absence of any Black teachers for many years to come. This tradeoff pattern repeated itself again and again throughout the years described in this study.

As Blacks were hired by the school board and their numbers increased they exerted internal pressure on the Board of Education. This pressure, coupled with some external pressures, resulted in the hiring of Blacks for higher positions, such as guidance counselor and principal. The field of guidance counseling remained closed to Blacks until 1960. The first Black counselor was assigned to a Black school in the Hill District. There were no Black principals until 1955. The first Black principal was assigned to a Black elementary school which was also in the Hill. This practice of assigning Blacks to Black schools before they were allowed to work elsewhere was to continue until the 1960s.

Systematic discrimination was also practiced in the employment of Black professionals for the central administrative staff of the Board of Education. The Board did not hire its first Black central-staff member until 1964. Even after that date the Board of Education continued to discriminate against Blacks as central-staff members. Not until the 1970s did the percentage of Blacks employed on the central staff approach the percentage of Blacks in the general population of Pittsburgh.

The internal pressure exerted on the Board by the increased number of Black professional employees also caused changes that benefited Black students. Some of these changes were evidenced in better treatment of Black students, better opportunities for Black athletes, better student counseling practices, more courses relating to the experiences of Black youngsters, and the removal of offensive books (such as *Little Black Sambo*) from libraries and classrooms.

It is evident that Blacks were discriminated against by the Pittsburgh Board of Public Education. It is also evident that the pattern of discrimination was not always the same. It changed over time. Sometimes it was very subtle and difficult to identify; at other times it was open and blatant. While the practices changed, the policy of discrimination remained the same.

Children in playground at A. Leo Weil School

Information Sources

Formal Documents

Bennett, Lerone Jr. *Before the Mayflower*. Baltimore: Penguin Books, 1962.

Betten, Neil, and Mohl, Raymond A. "The Evolution of Racism in a Northern Industrial City, 1906-1940; A Case Study of Gary, Indiana." *Journal of Negro History* 59 (1974): 51-64.

Brewer, James. *Robert L. Vann and The Pittsburgh Courier*. Unpublished master's thesis, University of Pittsburgh, 1941.

Buni, Andrew. *Robert L. Vann of The Pittsburgh Courier*. Pittsburgh: University of Pittsburgh Press, 1974.

Culver, Dwight, W. "Racial Desegregation in Education in Indiana." *Journal of Negro Education* 3 (1954): 296-302.

Darden, Joe T. *Afro Americans in Pittsburgh: The Residential Segregation of a People*. Lexington, Mass.: D.C. Heath: 1973.

Editorial. "Negro Teachers and Desegregation of Public Schools." *Journal of Negro Education* 2 (1953), 95-101.

Epstein, Abraham. *The Negro Migrant in Pittsburgh*. Unpublished master's thesis, University of Pittsburgh, 1918.

Gottlieb, Peter. *Making Their Own Way: Southern Blacks Migration to Pittsburgh 1916-1930*. Unpublished doctoral dissertation, University of Pittsburgh, 1977.

Meltzer, Milton, ed. *In Their Own Words—A History of the American Negro, 1865-1916*. New York: Thomas Y. Crowell: 1965.

Osofsky, Gilbert. *Harlem: The Making of a Ghetto*. New York: Harper § Row, 1963.

Pennsylvania Human Relations Commission. "The Chester Case." *Integrated Education* 5, no.1 (February 1965): 15-25.

Record, C. Wilson. "School Board and Negro Teachers in California." *Integrated Education* 1, no.2 (april 1963): 20- 22.

Tyack, David. *The One Best System: A History of American Urban Education*. Cambridge, Mass.: Harvard University Press, 1974.

Wilmoth, Ann G. *Pittsburgh and the Blacks: A Short History 1780-1875*. Unpublished doctoral dissertation, The Pennsylvania State University, 1975.

Wilson, Erasmus. *Standard History of Pittsburgh, Pennsylvania*. Chicago: H.R. Cornell, 1898.

Archival Documents

Brown, Wilhelmina Byrd, wife of Judge Homer S. Brown, personal papers.

Commission on Human Relations Report, 1969-72. Pittsburgh

"Hearings Before the Select Committee on Equal Educational Opportunity of the United States Senate, Ninety First Congress, Second Session, On Equal Educational Opportunity." Washington, D.C.: Government Printing Office, 1970.

McCoy, William Daniel. *History of Pittsburgh Public Schools to 1942*. (Unpublished notes of October 1959). Archives of an Industrial Society, Hillman Library, University of Pittsburgh.

NAACP, Pittsburgh Branch. Files located in the Archives of an Industrial Society, Hillman Library, University of Pittsburgh.

Pittsburgh Board of Public Education

- Office of Attendance
- Office of Statistics
- Office of Personnel

Pittsburgh Board of Public Education. Minutes of Board Meetings located in the Archives of an Industrial Society, University of Pittsburgh, Hillman Library.

"Quest for Racial Equality in the Pittsburgh Public Schools." The Annual Report for 1965; Board of Education, Pittsburgh, Pennsylvania, 1965.

"Report of the Pennsylvania State Temporary Commission on Urban Colored Population." Harrisburg: Commonwealth of Pennsylvania, January 1943.

"Social Condition of the Negro in the Hill." Urban League of Pittsburgh, 1930.

"Status of Education of Negroes in Pittsburgh, 1963-64." The Pittsburgh Human Relations Commission, 1964.

"Study of the Educational Department of the Pittsburgh Public Schools." Pittsburgh Board of Public Education, 1928.

Urban League, Pittsburgh Branch. Files located in the Archives of an Industrial Society, Hillman Library, University of Pittsburgh.

Newspaper Articles

The Bulletin Index, Pittsburgh, Pennsylvania: April 22, 1937.

The Pittsburgh Courier, Pittsburgh, Pennsylvania:

- Multiple issues 1926-1973.
- February 2, 1935
- March 9, 1935
- May 1, 1937

- May 8, 1937
- August 26, 1950
- January 30, 1954
- June 25, 1955
- September 5, 1964
- August 6, 1966
- June 19, 1976

The Pittsburgh Post-Gazette, Pittsburgh, Pennsylvania:

- April 23, W 5 1
- June 23, 1970

The Pittsburgh Press, Pittsburgh, Pennsylvania:

- Multiple issues 1916-1950.
- April 25, 1937
- June 3, 1937
- June 6, 1976

The Pittsburgh Sun Telegraph, Pittsburgh, Pennsylvania: April 25, 1937

Oral Interviews

Alston, Waunetta, 1973
Biggs, Irv, 1976
Blanding, John, 1970-73
Blanding, Martha, 1970-73
Bolden, Frank, 1973-75
Brevard, Doris G., 1973
Brewer, John, 1976
Brown, Carl, 1973-78
Brown, Frances, 1973
Brown, Homer, 1975
Brown, Wilhemena, 1973
Calloway, Elmo, 1973
Cook, Robert, 1973
Currington, Nan, 1973
Cyrus, Norine, 1973-1974
Dean, James, 1970-73
Epperson, David, 1978
Faison, Helen, 1973
Fisher, William, 1973
Fox, Alma, 1975-1977
Fulwylie, Christine, 1973

Gilliard, Audia Mae, 1973
Golden, Lois, 1973
Green, William, 1973
Guice, Ollie Mae, 1973
Harris, Jody, 1973-1975
Holly, Roosevelt, 1973
Huddle, Ernest, 1973
Jones, Richard F., 1973-1975
Kerr, Tom, 1973
Latimer, Bee, 1974
Latimer, Harry, 1974
LeVelle, Robert, 1973-1975
Lewis, John, 1973
Milliones, Margaret, 1973-1975
Morgart, John, 1973
Morrison, Helen Miller, 1973
Mungin, Bob, 1973
McAhaffey, Bee, 1974
McClain, Herman, 1973
McNairy, Gladys, 1978
McNutt, Charles, date unknown

Nicholson, William, 1973
Parks, Ernestine, 1973
Parrish, Herb, 1973
Pearce, Georgine, 1973
Peeler, Dorothea, 1973
Peeler, Lawrence, 1973-1978
Proctor, Ralph Sr., 1970-1974
Proctor, Ruby, 1970-1974
Robinson, Florine, 1973
Stallings, Hazel, 1973
Stone, Mary Louise, 1973, 1976

Sumpter, Myrna, 1973
Thompson, Eloise B., 1973
Vasser, Ted, 1973
Wade, Alice Bernice, 1973
Wade, Gertrude, 1973, 1976
Whedbee, Maxine, 1973
White, Willa, 1973
Wilkerson, Herbert, 1975, 1977
Williams, Paul, 1973
Woods, Leo, 1973
Young, John, 1973

Acknowledgements

There are many people who helped me on this project. I'd like to thank all of them for their contributions—my typist and dear friend who struggled with me through what must have seemed like endless changes and revisions; my late friend, Dr. Norman Dixon, whose devotion to equal education for Blacks led to my focusing on this particular project; Dr. Laurence Glasco, my thesis advisor, who encouraged this project and directed the major changes; Dr. Peter Karsten, who was always ready to help when I called; Dr. David Montgomery, whose valuable insights and suggestions helped to move the project along; Dr. Arthur Tuden, my long-time friend, who has established the best student-professor relationship I have ever witnessed, and who was always there to listen, to advise and to give that extra push. My thanks also go to the many teachers, civil-rights activists and other Pittsburgh residents who very generously consented to my persistent interviews. To my loved ones, who bore with me through the long process of my completing this dissertation, I also give my heartfelt thanks . Finally, to Ralph and Ruby Proctor, my parents, who gave years of love, support and understanding and whose only request was that I do my best, I dedicate this dissertation to you with all my love. Thank you.

About the Author

R alph Proctor, Jr., was born and raised in The Hill, the largest Black enclave in Pittsburgh Pennsylvania. He has an earned PhD in History, from The University of Pittsburgh. He is a pioneer in the use of Oral History at the University level, and used that technique as the primary research tool for his dissertation. That document is widely quoted and was the basis of two Federal lawsuits against segregated school systems in the United States.

Proctor is also a pioneer in the field of radio and television, in Pittsburgh, Pennsylvania, having been the producer/host of *Black Horizons*, a television program focusing on the Black Community. The program was the second such show in America and aired on WQED television. He also was the producer and host of five other radio and television programs in Pittsburgh.

He has taught a variety of subjects—including History, Ethnic Studies and African Art—at the university level for more than fifty years. He has taught at six colleges and universities in the United States and Korea. He has done much research on Blacks in the United States and has published *Voices from the Firing Line,* a memoir about the civil rights movement in Pittsburgh.

A recognized expert in African art, Proctor has published *The African Art Lover's Guide to Collecting* and *African Images to Color*. He has mounted numerous African art exhibitions; served as a consultant on African American history and African Art; has appeared on numerous radio and television shows, and has been featured in numerous magazine and newspaper articles. He is a world traveler and has conducted an African Art and Culture tour to West Africa.

Learning Moments Press is the publishing arm of the Scholar-Practitioner Nexus, an online community of individuals committed to the quality of education. Learning Moments Press features three series of books.

The Wisdom of Practice Series showcases the work of individuals who illuminate the complexities of practice as they strive to fulfill the purpose of their profession.

The Wisdom of Life Series offers insightful reflections on significant life events that challenge the meaning of one's life, one's sense of self, and one's place in the world.

The Social Context Series showcases the work of individuals who illuminate the macro socio-economic-political contexts within which education policy and practice are enacted.

Cooligraphy artist Daniel Nie created the logo for Learning Moments Press by combining two symbol systems. Following the principles of ancient Asian symbols, Daniel framed the logo with the initials of Learning Moments Press. Within this frame, he has replicated the Adinkra symbol for Sankofa as interpreted by graphic artists at the Documents and Design Company. As explained by Wikipedia, Adinkra is a writing system of the Akan culture of West Africa. Sankofa symbolizes taking from the past what is good and bringing it into the present in order to make positive progress through the benevolent use of knowledge. Inherent in this philosophy is the belief that the past illuminates the present and that the search for knowledge is a life-long process.